FOUR CULTURES OF THE WEST

FOUR CULTURES OF THE WEST

JOHN W. O'MALLEY

THE BELKNAP PRESS OF
HARVARD UNIVERSITY PRESS
Cambridge, Massachusetts
London, England
2004

Printed in the United States of America

A version of this book was presented at the First Biennial Blessed Pope John XXIII Lecture Series in Theology and Culture at the University of Notre Dame in 2002.

Library of Congress Cataloging-in-Publication Data

O'Malley, John W.
Four cultures of the West / John W. O'Malley.
p. cm.
Includes bibliographical references and index.
ISBN 0-674-01498-7 (alk. paper)
1. Civilization, Western—History. I. Title.

CB245.045 2004
909′.0982—dc22
2004047730

For my colleagues at Weston Jesuit School of Theology

Contents

FOUR CULTURES OF THE WEST

Today the text we are to study is the book of our own experience.

—*Bernard of Clairvaux, Homily 3 on the Song of Solomon*

INTRODUCTION

Athens and Jerusalem

THIS BOOK IS about four phenomena in the history of the West. I call them cultures. In illustrating their characteristics I make large use of my specialty, the history of Christianity. I have written the book for anyone interested in either of those two histories, which for long periods were in fact almost indistinguishable from each other. I have written it, therefore, for specialists, for students, and for the general reader. Specialists will be familiar with the persons, issues, and movements I discuss, but I hope that my approach will stimulate them to think about these subjects in a new way. Students and the general reader may initially be bewildered by the swirl of names they encounter for the first time, or at least have never studied in any depth, but I believe they will profit from the book. Among other things, it provides a framework of interpretive categories. Moreover, the book is straightforward and iterative. Issues and persons keep reappearing, presented each time from a slightly different angle. If you miss them the first time, you will catch them the second or third. Educators, I think you, especially, will find the book worth reading.

The device I use for approaching my subject is a construct: four cultures. As the title indicates, the book is first and foremost about those cultures. With them I hold up for appreciation phenomena deeply embedded in the history of the West, so deeply embedded, in fact, that we sometimes become oblivious to their import. These phenomena are with us still, though in radically transformed ways. The purpose of the book is to make us less oblivious of them and thus more appreciative.

The idea of four cultures began to surface in my mind many years ago while I was in Rome working on a book about sermons preached in the Sistine Chapel during the Renaissance. They then helped me sort out in a somewhat new way the tangle of issues raised by another area of my research, the Protestant-Catholic conflicts of the sixteenth century. In my book on the Sistine sermons I had to deal directly with the relationship between "the new learning" of humanism and its medieval antecedent (and sometimes enemy), Scholasticism. That relationship was in fact what my book was all about, as I traced the transformative effect that the introduction of humanist rhetoric had on the mood, aim, religious and cultural sensibilities, and even content of preaching, moving it from its medieval styles to a style quite different. I began to see something with startlingly new clarity: *how* things were said was just as important as *what* was said, even though the *how* and the *what* could never be neatly separated.

When I began to study the Reformation, I was struck by the same thing. In the famous debate between Erasmus and Luther on free will, the difference seemed to me more profound and far-reaching than their respective ideas on free will and grace. They talked in very different styles. *How* they spoke was as different as *what* they said. Did not this difference in style point to more profound differences? Were they not, while arguing from the same texts, working out of irreconcilable assumptions? Working, it increasingly began to seem to me, out of different cultures?

I was also interested in questions like these because my training as a Jesuit, very old-fashioned, had been a self-conscious replay and amalgam of the humanistic and Scholastic traditions as they were embodied in educational programs. I was curious to understand better what had happened to me in the process. I knew there was something more involved than the facile explanation that humanist eloquence provided adornment for Scholastic content. Did not the latter also have form—or style? Did not the former have content? It was the style issue, however, that I increasingly saw as critical.

These were the origins of the book. Despite encouragement from friends and colleagues, I long hesitated to write it. I am fond of my cultures, but I am also aware of my limitations, and I am, like most historians, skeptical of grand schemes. I finally decided to go ahead with the project because I trusted readers to have the good sense to take it for what I intend it to be—not a pronouncement from on high but a stimulus to discussion and an invitation to reflection. It is an essay in the basic sense of that word—an attempt, a sortie.

I see the cultures originating, as to be expected, in the ancient Mediterranean world of "Athens and Jerusalem." They consisted in (1) the culture of Isaiah and Jeremiah the prophets; (2) the culture of Plato and Aristotle the philosophers and scientists; (3) the culture of Homer and Isocrates, of Virgil and Cicero, the culture of poets and dramatists, of orators and statesmen; and finally, (4) the culture of Phidias, Polycletus, Praxiteles, and countless other artists, artisans, and architects, the culture of art and performance.

The cultures migrated through time and space from the Roman world of early Christianity into the Middle Ages. Between the eleventh and the sixteenth centuries, through a series of eureka-experiences, what we call renaissances and reformations, they achieved a new coherence and a new force that propelled them into the modern world.

I will describe these special moments in some detail and try to persuade you of their significance. Then I will give particular attention to the sixteenth century, when the cultures, by confronting and doing battle with one another under the cover of religious polemics, made even more manifest their special traits. It is the century of towering protagonists—Luther, Erasmus, Michelangelo, and the theologians of the Council of Trent. It is the century that I know best, and it is the century that lies at the center of this book. I will swiftly move closer to the present without trying to do more than make a few observations about how the cultures, greatly modified of course and secularized, have fared particularly in North America. I invite readers to discern, if they feel so disposed, where in their own history and milieus the cultures have import and impact.

In the late second and early third century the fierce Christian apologist and polemicist Tertullian asked the question that provides the basic structure for the way I develop my theses about the cultures: What, he asked, has Athens to do with Jerusalem?[1] That is, what has human culture to do with the transcendent claims of Judaism and Christianity? Nothing at all, was Tertullian's answer. Others both before and after disagreed with him, affirming in either theory or action that Athens and Jerusalem were on some level compatible. Tertullian himself was far from consistent on the point, but he was certainly not the only person to give the same negative answer, often with similar inconsistencies.

My essay, then, is an attempt to trace both negative and affirmative answers to Tertullian's question. It is not, however, about "Christ and culture." It is not a theological interpretation of the history of the West. It makes use of religion to get into better focus certain aspects of Western history, certain modalities of Western intelligence, that have a stunningly long history stretching from ancient times until today.

The book, unfashionable in several ways, is in our postmodern era especially unfashionable in trying to sketch a Big Picture. My training in medieval philosophy alerted me early on to the problem of "universals," that is, of general concepts and their relationship to concrete particulars, a problem of which modern philosophy in different terms has made us again acutely aware. From historians, moreover, Big Pictures win big criticism.

Though wary, I nonetheless have faith in the utility of the cultures. On one level the cultures are, to be sure, fictions, but on another they are sufficiently grounded in "what happened" to be more than fictions. They are in my opinion readily discernible in the past and the present, so that for many readers I will be doing little more than recalling them to mind or raising awareness of them by pointing out some of their manifestations. They are not exotic. To my knowledge, however, no one has proposed them in quite the way I do.

By relating the cultures to Tertullian's question, I am able to provide a road map through some areas of Western history. With such a question determining which roads get put on the map, I of course make religion the central highway. I present the cultures principally as they manifest themselves in the history of Christianity. Given my background, I could not write the book in any other way, nor would I want to. Recent international events have made devastatingly clear how important religion is as a force in the world and how we neglect studying it to our own peril.

I will, then, talk mostly about religious figures and movements, yet I will do so insofar as they are expressions of the "cultures." By that term I mean four large, self-validating configurations of symbols, values, temperaments, patterns of thinking, feeling, and behaving, and patterns of discourse. I mean especially configurations of patterns of discourse and thus expressions of *style* in the profoundest sense of the word. *Le style, c'est l'homme même.*

As important as I believe the four cultures are, I do not call them *the* four cultures. They are capacious but not all-inclusive. They do not take account of Celtic or Germanic cultures. They take no account of what we today might call business culture, the culture of the marketplace and the stock exchange. They take no account of legions of other things. Nor do they easily correlate with every important religious figure. I do not find an obvious place among the cultures, for instance, for Ignatius of Loyola, the founder of my own religious order. If you imagine Western civilization as a vast ocean, you might imagine the four cultures as four Gulf Streams flowing through it. The streams help us understand many phenomena, but they are not the ocean.

In the section that follows I give a thumbnail description of each of the cultures and in so doing almost perforce stress their differences, even their occasional hostility to one another. But for the most part the cultures tend to blend together, borrow from each other, and they have often supported one another almost to the point of being indistinguishable, seemingly unaware that there might be a level at which they were incommensurable. If the sixteenth century marked their most vicious confrontation, the following century manifested one of their most notable reconciliations. The cultures are rivals. They are also partners.

Four Cultures

1. PROPHETIC CULTURE

What has Athens to do with Jerusalem? In this book I take Jerusalem to stand for one aspect (only one) of the Judeo-Christian tradition: its insistence on the incomprehensibility, the transcendence, the utter otherness of God. I call this the prophetic culture. "For my thoughts are not your thoughts, neither are my ways your ways," said Yahweh through Isaiah. Thus spoke the Holy One, who writes straight with crooked lines. "Has not God made foolish the wisdom of this world?" asked Paul. The reasonings of the philosophers are, in this Jerusalem, senseless babble. For Luther reason (Aristotle) was a whore that repelled him—he staked his claim on Scripture alone. For Kierkegaard there was no escaping the *Either/Or.*

This is the culture that must speak out. It is the culture of alienation, of protest, of standing apart because one can do no other. Here gather the Puritans and the Jansenists and all those given to crusades. Fundamentalists both religious and secular are comfortable here. This is the culture of the martyr (and the fanatic). It is the culture, above all, of the reformer decrying injustice and corruption in high places. It wills to transform a corrupt and unfaithful status quo into the genuine article. Throughout history justice has been its watchword, along with variants like righteousness and justification. Freedom is also one of its favorite words. This is the culture that makes the greatest purity claims and that unmasks as abomination what others welcome as the normal give-and-take of life. It cannot compromise. Rallies and protests, yes. The negotiating table, never!

If this culture must decry its times, it must also hold out promise of better times to come: "For behold, darkness shall cover the earth, and thick darkness the peoples; but the Lord will arise upon you and his glory will be seen upon you." It is therefore the culture of great expectations, expectations that surpass anything that seems humanly possible. The Book of Revelation promised "a new heaven and a new earth." Martin Luther King, Jr., held out a more circumscribed but seemingly just as unattainable eventuality: "I have a dream."

This culture appeals to a higher standard, revealed to the few, hidden from the many. God wills it. In a post-Enlightenment, more secularized context the standard will take the form of an unquestionable First Principle, often in rights-language—the Right to Life or the Right to Choose. It will rally the oppressed: "Workers of the world, unite." Freedom, no more chains.

Because the standard is beyond argument, this culture must state boldly, even shout its claims, as does the herald of both good and bad news. Its mode of discourse is the imperative: Repent! It finds form in manifestoes. It must sometimes make noise. Carrie Nation, campaigning against the evils of alcohol, described herself as "a bulldog running along at the feet of Jesus, barking at what he doesn't like."

Prophets proclaim their message through the stark dichotomies of God/Satan, Christ/Anti-Christ, spirit/flesh, grace/free will, Good/Bad, patriot/traitor, capitalism/any-other-system, politically correct/politically incorrect. Choose, for between these extremes there is no common ground. This culture looks to the Jesus who said he had come to bring not peace but the sword and to set son against father and daughter against mother. The Anabaptists at Münster could not have taken this message more literally when in 1534 they proclaimed death by sword for all the ungodly.

Yet under its wings this culture also gathers the gentle like Dorothy Day, Dietrich Bonhoeffer, and Oscar Romero. The "Swiss Brethren," Anabaptists of a stripe altogether different from the belligerents of Münster, looked to the Jesus who said his kingdom was not of this world, and they therefore abstained from this world as far as they could. Their proclamation took the form of withdrawal into an other-worldly world constructed for the purpose. They were prophets through their witness. Their very silence and passivity proclaimed their truth as loudly as words. Paradoxes like this are also characteristic of the prophetic style.

No matter what form the proclamation takes, the message demands conversion, reform, and utter commitment. Paul struck to the ground on his way to Damascus provides the paradigm for the altogether radical and sometimes instantaneous reversal of values that conversion effects, as the persecutor stepped forth as the apostle. This is the culture congenial for those whom William James described as "the twice-born."

Pope Gregory VII (1073–1085), proposing a program to set medieval society on its head, provides a striking paradigm for the reformer wholly intent upon putting things right, no matter what the cost. Bound like the prophet "to cry aloud and spare not" (Isa. 58.11), Gregory feared he would fail in his mission if, like a dumb dog, he was afraid to bark (Isa. 56.10). This urgency led him to take on the most powerful and prestigious figure of the day, the "Roman" (that is, the German) emperor. He found in the canonical legislation of the early church (genuine and forged) the standard, long lost from view, for the way things were supposed to be. He invoked ancient sources to justify his revolution. As is true of so many revolutions, Gregory fought this one in the name of a restoration of the good old days, unaware that because society had changed so radically from those days, what he proposed had, in its profoundest implications, never been heard of before.

The "Gregorian Reform" that bears his name, that great upheaval also known as the "Investiture Controversy," is a specially defining moment for the prophetic culture in the West. Gregory and his entourage gave unwitting first form to that disruptive and strident peculiarity of Western Christianity that eventually spawned its secular counterparts: the idea that the church as an institution could, and under certain circumstances should, be redone to a degree and in a way that profoundly defied the status quo and received wisdom. From the past they reinvented, Gregory and his colleagues tried to construct the future.

By defining reform as institutional in its object and sweeping in its scope, they gave the prophetic culture an articulation in word and deed that it had not known before and that injected it in a new and especially forceful way into the subsequent history of the West. Much of that history could indeed be written under the rubrics of reforms and reformations.

In this culture the second defining figure for the West was Luther. He knew nothing about Gregory, yet their prophetic profiles are remarkably similar. Luther, however, rewrote the book on what it means to be a prophet simply by turning out to be a historical figure of mythic proportions in modern Western imagination. Everybody has heard of him. He made courage in fighting for systemic change perhaps the most distinctively Western of all the virtues. Though some cannot abide him, he is the great hero of the modern West: "Here I stand. I can do no other." He transposed prophecy to a new key and made it a tune to be played *fortissimo.*

In broad outline this is what I mean by the prophetic culture, the culture of Jerusalem. For convenience I will call it culture one. The other three cultures belong to Athens.

What about Athens? I take it not so much as a metaphor for some generic "human culture" as pointing in the first instance to the Athens of real history. My Athens is a metaphor grounded in real time and place. I thus see it as standing for three areas of accomplishment in "the glory that was Greece" that had an incalculable impact on the West. As indicated, I see it as standing for a certain style of learning, then for oratory and literature, and finally for art and performance.

There is no need to stress how profoundly each of these achievements, including their Roman articulations, interacted with Christianity from the earliest centuries. Paul in his speech on the Areopagus, as reported in Acts 17, seems to provide warrant for thinking that aspects of Athens, the secular city, might have something to do with Jerusalem, the sacred city: What you, Athenians, "worship as unknown, this I proclaim to you."

2. ACADEMIC/PROFESSIONAL CULTURE

The culture of Plato and Aristotle, the culture of a certain style of learning, is the aspect of Athens with which many people today are familiar, at least on a superficial level. No historical survey in almost any discipline can omit mention of these two giants who rightly dominate Raphael's famous fresco, "The School of Athens." Platonism in its various manifestations infiltrated into the thought patterns of the West from antiquity into modern times to such an extent that they became one, almost indistinguishable. The writings of the Fathers of the Church evince this influence, and even though Augustine repudiated "the Platonists," he could hardly have been more deeply affected by them. In what follows I take Plato's pervasiveness for granted. I also take for granted that other philosophers and thinkers from "the School of Athens" (and the School of Rome) influenced early Christians in important ways.

Aristotle emerged with startling brilliance with the translation into Latin of his full corpus in the High Middle Ages, after which he dominated the history of the sciences and other academic disciplines for centuries. More pertinent for us, the relationship of Athens to Jerusalem took on its medieval formulation as the relationship between "reason and revelation," which was nothing other than an abstract formulation of the relationship between Aristotle (for the most part) and the Bible. Aristotle was appreciated not only for his works on logic, ethics, and metaphysics but also for those on animals, the heavenly bodies, and other natural phenomena—on "natural philosophy." The relationship of Athens to Jerusalem could thus be expressed, anachronistically, as that between science and religion. Could this Athens and this Jerusalem at least in certain important aspects be reconciled, even though the former city was this-worldly, the latter other-worldly? Many practitioners in the medieval universities believed reconciliation was possible up to a point.

Here, however, I am interested not in how the relationship between Aristotle and the Bible was variously understood in the different "schools" or in the ideas and philosophical systems of Plato and Aristotle but in a certain style of learning and discoursing that they launched and that received its most rigorous, reflective, and aggressive form in the universities of the Middle Ages. That style is the analytical, questing and questioning, restless and relentless style in which we in academe are today immersed. It is the style of learning that is never satisfied, that is critical of every wisdom, that is insatiably eager to ask the further question, and that is ever ready to propose yet another perspective. It is the style of learning that is almost by definition agonistic and contentious. It is the style that holds in highest honor sound argument.

Plato's Socrates probed, almost taunted, his interlocutors with questions that looked to a dispassionate analysis of the subject at issue. What is virtue? What is justice? But it was with Aristotle that the pursuit was carried forward into almost every branch of knowledge, with massive codification of observations about the physical world and of speculation about the soul and the metaphysical composition of the universe. Especially impressive were codifications of logic, dialectic, and rhetoric, that is, of the processes of human discourse and of reasoning themselves. Boethius transmitted to the Middle Ages in Latin translation half of Aristotle's works on logic, which were studied and appropriated long before the rest of the corpus became available. These works in particular grounded academic culture in its fundamental characteristic and great glory: reliance on solid evidence and close reasoning.

If the style of discourse of the prophetic culture is the shout, the proclamation, the lament, the command, the bark, the paradox, then the style of this culture is the logical, rigorous, left-brain discourse that moves to resolution. As in the prophetic culture, nothing soft is tolerated here. But whereas the former culture glories in dichotomies at the very highest level of generalization, such as good and bad, God and mammon, this culture glories in close examination of particulars that lead to precise distinctions formulated in sharply defined concepts. Such concepts form the basis for further questions, which put one on the road, perhaps, to understanding or constructing a whole system or synthesis.

Perhaps the greatest and most lasting institutional achievement of the Middle Ages was the creation of the university, which in its basic structures and ethos, despite many vicissitudes through eight centuries, has retained a remarkable identity. The university stimulated, produced, and provided a home for a style of learning that has persisted into the present and only gained strength and credibility in the past hundred years. That is the style of the learned specialist, publicly certified, decked out with degrees, fluent in specialized vocabulary and in highly stylized methods of arguing. Whereas the Gregorian Reform is a great turning point in the history of prophetic culture, the recovery of Aristotle and the foundation of the universities is a momentous turning point here.

The discovery of the texts of Aristotle in the twelfth century helped stimulate the creation of the university, and Aristotle's works on logic and dialectics powerfully stimulated the development of the institution's intellectual style. The product was what we know as Scholasticism, that is, learning in the scholastic or academic manner, the learning of university folk. To pursue this learning one had to spend years "in the schools," which now had set curricula, approved textbooks, formal examinations, faculties organized according to disciplines or professions such as law and medicine, and finally, the public certification of degrees—Bachelor of Arts, Master of Arts, Doctor of Medicine, Doctor of Philosophy.

This culture differs radically from culture one in that it has had a massive institutional embodiment from the thirteenth century forward. From then onward it would be almost impossible to speak of this culture without speaking about the university or analogous institutions. It finds its most appropriate home in the classroom, the laboratory, the library, the think tank, the research institute, the closed meetings of learned societies. These are its cloisters.

Through the centuries the universities abandoned the ideas of Aristotle and other ancient thinkers that for centuries provided much of the content of academic discourse. But the culture the medieval Scholastics created out of them has only become more normative. This has of course not been a straight-line development since the thirteenth century. In the late nineteenth and twentieth centuries, and especially in the past fifty years since World War II, the universities have increasingly claimed for themselves the territory of traditional "high culture." They have even claimed certain fields that society would once have considered low culture, for they have long offered degrees in business and agriculture.

This is academic culture, which I call culture two. The story of culture two might be called the triumph of the philosophers ("scientists"), and it is how we tend to read Western intellectual history—Descartes, Galileo, Kant, Freud, Einstein, Derrida. We read it as if Plato's besting the Sophists in argument went unchallenged and led from that point, or at least from Aristotle, right into the astrophysicist's laboratory. But there is another story, just as important but less familiar today.

3. HUMANISTIC CULTURE

This is the story of great literature and of the modes in which it was interpreted and studied. Recent generations have forgotten, or have never been told, that Plato and Aristotle lost the battle to educate the youth of the Greco-Roman world. It was won by persons like Isocrates who built upon foundations the Sophists had to a great extent laid. Cicero, Virgil, St. Ambrose, and St. Augustine were trained in the skills and ideals set forth not by Plato and Aristotle or the other philosophers of Athens but by those deriving from the other tradition based on literature. They had an education steeped in poetry, drama, history, and rhetoric (oratory)—what would come to be called a humanistic education. Of course after their formal schooling some of them became profoundly learned in the teaching of the Platonists, the Aristotelians, the Stoics, and others, but not so deeply as to lose their grounding in the culture in which they were brought up.

The literary culture persisted in eclectic and sometimes fragmented form into the Middle Ages, reaching a new climax in the twelfth century with St. Bernard and his Cistercian colleagues, just as the sister/rival culture of the universities was beginning to assert itself. This was the culture serenely in possession in the West until the universities appeared.

It was this culture that the humanists of the Renaissance powerfully reinstated when they revived ancient literary genres and made literature the center of the curriculum. That reinstatement is the original reason for calling the period Renaissance. The Renaissance was the eureka-moment for culture three, as it now had a powerful foil against which to understand itself, the university. The implicit watchword for culture two was good argument. The quite explicit watchword for culture three was "good literature" *(bonae litterae).* By that expression the humanists meant the literary masterpieces of Greek and Latin antiquity, but by a curious symbiosis they and their contemporaries made some of the first lasting contributions to the great corpus of vernacular masterpieces that has continued to expand almost exponentially down to the present.

This literary culture prevailed in the Western world into the twentieth century largely because, as culture two did with the university, the humanists also created a powerful machine of indoctrination and propagation, the humanistic secondary school, which was variously known as the *Gymnasium,* the *Lycée,* the *Liceo,* the Public School (in England), the Grammar School or the Latin School, and, eventually, the Young Ladies' Academy. It also prevailed because by the seventeenth century it had invaded and in some cases transformed the so-called Arts faculty of the universities. Like culture two, then, culture three for long periods of its history needs to be looked at in relationship to its institutional expressions.

The ideals held high in this culture were embodied and exemplified in literature, which begins with poetry. Homer was the schoolmaster of Greece. In poetry the reasons of the heart prevail, in a form of discourse that is more circular than linear. If culture two seeks clear-cut definition, this culture, at least in this particular aspect, glories in ambiguity, in rich layers of meaning. Whatever

Blake's "Sick Rose" is about, it is not primarily about a diseased plant. For Christians Scripture becomes a book in which each verse or section is happily laden with multiple senses, one as valid as the other. Dante self-consciously constructed the *Commedia* to yield a fourfold meaning.

Educators in this tradition often tended to a didactic approach to "good letters," but the better among them saw further that literature reflects the complexities of life and the murky darkness in which our choices must sometimes be made. It is a mirror held up to life that helps us make sense of our experience and sparks our moral imagination. Even as "the classics" became in recent centuries ever more relegated to specialists in Latin and Greek, the novel and the play assumed for the heirs of this tradition the status of wisdom literature. They gave aesthetic pleasure, but even as they did so they acted as gentle and persuasive invitations to look inward and to see ourselves and our dilemmas through other eyes. Huck Finn, Jim, Tom, and Aunt Polly reveal parts of ourselves.

In the educational program or *paideia* that propelled this cultural ideal, the other constitutive part besides poetry was rhetoric, that is, the art of public speaking. The orator, virtually synonymous with the statesman or politician, is concerned with contingencies. Is war required of us *now*, under *these* circumstances? He argues, therefore, from probabilities to attain a solution not certain but more likely of success than its alternatives. Like the poet, then, the statesman deals with ambiguities, very unlike the protagonist from culture two, who traditionally argued from principles to attain a truth certain and proved to be such; cultures two and three represent, thus, two different approaches to problem-solving. Like the prophet of culture one, the statesman of culture three wants to change society for the better, but to do so he seeks common ground and knows that to attain his end he must be astute in compromise. He does not shun the negotiating table. If the prophet looks to the Jesus who came to bring the sword, the statesman looks to Jesus, Prince of Peace.

The basic values giving shape and coherence to this aspect of the culture were operative from the beginning and were often explicit. Isocrates, a younger contemporary of Plato, was much influenced by the Sophists. Basically a teacher of oratory, he was stung by Plato's criticisms. He responded by trying to make the Sophistic tradition intellectually and morally responsible. As an educator, he judged the education Plato envisaged as impractical, for it required most of the years of a man's life and also isolated him from the urgent concerns of society. It produced ivory-tower intellectuals, not the men of action that society needed, not men given to a life of service for the public good. The kind of learning that Aristotle later represented, especially in his "natural philosophy," was even further removed from life in the polis. It dealt not with human issues but with speculation about animals and the physical world.

Whereas the culture represented by Plato and Aristotle ends up pursuing with special zeal Truth, the culture represented by Isocrates and his followers is more intent upon the Good. The pursuit of Truth in the former culture leads to ever more little truths, whereas the latter placidly ruminates on a few fundamental values that hardly need arguing. Who would deny that love makes the world go around? Or who would deny that loyalty to family, friends, and country is admirable, that injustice is heinous, treachery worse?

This culture does not particularly prize "original thought" as such (it might even hold it suspect), but it does prize the wisdom that knows how to make old truths effective in new ways for the common good. "Mrs. Roosevelt was not a profound thinker," said one of her biographers, "nor was she very original in the philosophical positions she took. . . . She expanded on existing ideas and applied them to current issues. . . . Despite her pragmatism, she lived all her life according to a set of absolute standards, which derived from principles of honesty and justice and the teachings of Christ. Social Christianity and a fundamental belief in democracy were the bases of her philosophy."[2] With patience and courage she chaired the committee that in 1948 produced the landmark United Nations' Universal Declaration of Human Rights.

Human issues dealt with in a human way was Isocrates's goal, and the human way was the way of human speech, that gift of the gods that distinguished human beings from animals. The burden of human speech was to convey the noble and uplifting ideals that bind society together and, by touching human affect, to kindle admiration for them and profound dedication. Eloquence was, then, a deep-seated value in this culture. But it was so because it was geared to the common good. At the center of culture three, therefore, was a moral imperative. Its schools looked as much to formation in upright character as to the acquisition of skills and knowledge. This culture is the culture of humane rumination and civic responsibility.

It might sometimes seem as though I am presuming that all great literary figures in the West, at least in the Middle Ages and Renaissance, were direct expressions of traditions traceable back to classical antiquity. Yet even for Petrarch, "the father of humanism," the dependency is clearest only for his Latin works, which nobody reads today. For Dante, and then for Shakespeare and others, direct dependency is even more tenuous. Nonetheless, the traditions of vernacular literature represented by Petrarch, Dante, and Shakespeare were in part shaped, sometimes profoundly, by the classical heritage.

This is, then, that "humanistic" culture that at least down to the middle of the last century formed most men and, after the seventeenth century, practically all women in the Western world who had the opportunity for formal schooling. The schooling did not in and of itself produce the great literature that is constitutive of culture three, yet it was a crucial part of the circumstances that did. In the public sphere it produced windbags, just as culture two produced nerds. It also produced Franklin and Eleanor Roosevelt. It produced Winston Churchill, whose eloquence "marshaled the English language and sent it into battle." Its greatest religious or theological expression in relatively recent times was in the documents of the Second Vatican Council held in 1962–1965.

4. ARTISTIC CULTURE

This is the culture that expresses itself in ritual performance like coronation rites, graduation ceremonies, and Veterans' Day parades. It is the culture of dance, painting, sculpture, music, and architecture—activities or products without which, it seems, ritual performance cannot happen. But these activities and products are not simply adjuncts to ritual. They have a reality of their own.

When Tertullian posed his question, he almost certainly was not thinking about how Jerusalem related to such realities. But a close relationship was inevitable, given the highly visual nature of the Greco-Roman matrix into which Christianity was born. The Roman Empire was a world of public rituals and public spectacles—chariot races, gladiatorial contests, street performers, religious rites. With the great majority of the population illiterate and not even speaking Greek and Latin, the languages of the cultural elite, the cohesion of the empire rested upon the power of images, especially imperial portraits, to communicate authority and responsibility. It was through material culture that the inhabitants of the empire imbibed the myth of Rome's greatness and its sublime destiny. Through statuary, not a canonical scripture, they got to know the gods.

Into this intensely visual culture Christians were born, and of it they breathed all the days of their lives. In this situation Christianity itself would eventually be defined most strikingly through material culture. It was this culture that would touch most Christians most directly, for it was inseparable from public Christian worship.

Tertullian probably saw no need to revisit the Decalogue's prohibition of graven images. Yet Christian belief that Jesus, for all the claims of transcendency made about him, walked and talked, suffered and died as a human being living in a certain time and place almost inevitably and rather soon led to depictions of him, at first only symbolically, as in the pelican or the shepherd. The icon would eventually follow.

But it was worship that provided the door for the culture of the artist to enter. As the Christian communities grew in size, they needed more space in which to gather for a worship at whose center was the Eucharistic meal, which was developing into formal and, relatively soon, elaborate liturgies. The material culture of the ancient world burst into the Christian communities, however, in the early fourth century with the conversion of Constantine. The enthusiasm with which the bishops accepted Constantine's massive building program in their favor and then took it up on their own is astounding. They seem not to have had second thoughts. With the great buildings came the arts to adorn them and to make the ceremonies consonant with their new and often magnificent settings. Building houses of worship even grander than Solomon's Temple became the ideal.

Of the four cultures the first three are cultures of words. Except for music, this culture is mute. It communicates, but not in words. Jesus prescribed that his followers perform certain actions such as baptizing and doing in memory of him what he did at the Last Supper. Christian teachers, reflecting on these actions, came to name them sacraments, a synonym here for sign or symbol. The sacraments belong, as Aquinas and others have said, "in the category of sign" *(in genere signi).* Even though words are integral to their proper administration, the words are void if not accompanied by the appropriate action, such as the pouring of the water in baptism. The sacraments are *performed.*

The mass belongs preeminently in this culture, for it is essentially a mime. Although in Christian belief the mystery of Christ's death and resurrection is what is ultimately being celebrated, the action follows the pattern, highly ritualized, of the Last Supper: "Do this in memory of me." This means that, even more obviously than with the sacraments, the mass is a performance. It is "a sacred action" in which the props and techniques the performers use convey much of the meaning. I am referring to such things as the sacred vessels, vestments (costumes), incense, flowers, music, gestures, processions, and other movements (as almost a subdued dance), and of course words. The mass is thus play, for like play it takes us to another world, but it is play of the most serious kind, "deep play."

The words of the liturgy are unlike those in the other cultures for they are stylized for the sublimity of the occasion. They are not spontaneous. They are, for the most part, set and inviolable formulae, to be repeated time after time, age after age, without variation, as in a venerable drama. In their very invariability they paradoxically speak to the present moment. Even the homily delivered in the course of the liturgy is supposed to conform in style and ethos to the sacred action that is under way and of which it is a part.

The process by which the gatherings of the first Christians developed into highly formalized actions was gradual and obscure. In any case it led Christians to incorporate into their worship forms first developed outside Jerusalem, some of which would have been alien or even anathema to the worship of Jerusalem. Iconoclasm, which first flared up in an organized way in the East in the eighth century, erupted again in the West in the sixteenth, with cries of idolatry, paganism, and superstition hurled at those who venerated images and who seemed to put trust in "ceremonies." This was a defining moment for culture four. Not only did most Protestant groups attack the use of images and then often the images themselves, but they also abolished the Liturgy of the Hours and tended to strip the Eucharistic liturgy down to bare table and words, if not to abolish it altogether.

Catholics, once somewhat recovered from the shock, responded with an exuberant reassertion of the divinely sanctioned validity of "ceremonies" and images. They would henceforth pursue religious painting more self-consciously and deliberately, and they would promote church building and restoration in a newly programmatic way. Meanwhile, the new churches of the Reformation developed new forms of ritual and made use of some of the arts, especially music, in effective but usually quite different ways than did their Catholic counterparts.

This is culture four, a culture integral to the story of the West and a culture absolutely central to the story of Christianity. Yet art and performance are accorded little if any attention in "general" histories or even in traditional "church histories." This is a bad distortion. In many European cities churches are usually the first public buildings that strike our attention, as with the cathedral in Cologne, and they often define the city center, as with the Duomo in Florence. It is culture four that Christians directly experienced every week of their lives, or even more often, as they gathered to worship. The other cultures may have touched them in various ways. This one was ever before them.

The origins and much of the subsequent history especially of cultures two and three are, no doubt, elitist. Culture two, which since the thirteenth century has been predominantly the culture of the university, required until quite recently too much time and too much money to be open to any but a select few, a negligible percentage of the population. Culture three was the culture of "the gentleman" and then of the "gentle lady." Yet, with culture two somewhat of a special case, all four by their very nature have wanted in some way to touch large numbers of people, down to the most humble, and they generally wanted to touch them in profound, life-altering ways.

In this book I am concerned with four cultures only in their peculiarly Euro-American manifestations. Other civilizations obviously have their counterparts in cultures three and four, in literature and art/performance. They may even have rough equivalents of culture one, though without the sharp contours shaped in the West by the Judeo-Christian tradition of prophecy, except when influenced by it, as in Islam. They surely have scientific and even "academic" traditions, although the universities as they eventually unfolded, no matter what their initial debt to Islamic institutions, became characteristic of the West in the complexity and sophistication of their organization and in the intellectual dynamism constitutive of their style. For culture two the universities became the relentless agents that made that culture's Western embodiment distinctive.

I make my argument from case studies taken from Western Christianity. What about Byzantium, which was even more a direct heir to the four cultures? There the cultures do not display the same contours as in the West or the same relatively clear delineations from one another. Why?

I am not so foolish as to try to answer that question. Yet I will point out that with the infiltration of Germanic and other tribes into the Western part of the Roman Empire and the consequent transformation and even partial dissolution of institutions and traditions of culture, the West experienced a break and loss that the East did not (except, of course, in territories it altogether lost to Islam). The moments of special energy and self-definition of each of the cultures in the West happened with a eureka-experience when those institutions or traditions were rediscovered and then necessarily reshaped by being introduced into an altogether different civilization. The Gregorians rediscovered the ancient legal texts, the Scholastics the texts of Greek science, logic, ethics, medicine, and metaphysics, the Italian humanists the texts of ancient literature and educational ideals. The artists of the Renaissance rediscovered or at least viewed with new eyes the sculpture and other artifacts of Roman antiquity. They then had to face the onslaught of the Iconoclasts, who believed they were restoring the good old days of imageless worship.

These recovered memories provoked in the West a sense of historical discontinuity, of a serious gap between past and present. Once upon a time something was, then it was not, now it must be brought back. The restorationist impulse generated energy. To this day a sense of unbroken continuity is characteristic of Greek Orthodoxy, for in that church they still speak the language of the New Testament and of the early councils of the church. In the West the contrast between the then and the now forced a much stronger sense of something lost and now found again. As that something was reinstated, it was transformed. Part of the transformation consisted in the cultures having a sharper differentiation from one another in the West.

Partners and Rivals

At certain times and in certain situations, as I have indicated, that sense of sharp differentiation turned the cultures into rivals, sometimes on the conscious level, as in the debate between humanists and Scholastics in the sixteenth century. More than traces of that rivalry persist into the present in debates over the teaching of "the Humanities" and what they are supposed to accomplish in the face of scientific, professional, technological, and other "practical" training—indeed, in all the debates over the very purpose of education.

Even when the cultures live in peaceful coexistence with one another, each tends to understand the others on its own terms. Liturgy, for instance, belongs fundamentally in culture four, but the other three cultures can legitimately claim a part in it. More often, however, they try to take it captive and seize it for themselves. Culture one wants it as the bully pulpit, culture two as a classroom for instruction in orthodoxy, culture three as an expression of religious or religiously political solidarity within a given milieu. They understand it, in other words, through the lenses of their own culture, which means they misconstrue it. Liturgy thus provides an excellent example of how any given culture must distort the others into its own image and likeness, into its own value system, in order to make sense of it.

A more secular example can be found in the schools. Over the past hundred years the form and methods of culture two have gradually encroached upon the teaching of "the Humanities," the traditional matter of culture three. Teachers of that matter must now be trained and certified in culture two. Over time the university has appropriated the stuff of culture three, transforming it into another set of academic disciplines. Culture two did this not out of ill will but simply because it had to act according to its own nature. When Shakespeare makes an appearance at a meeting of the Modern Language Association of America, he finds himself not being read and enjoyed or being admired for his humane wisdom, but analyzed, debated, and deconstructed.

If only the English and Americans spoke the same language, Churchill complained. Wittgenstein made essentially the same point: if a lion could talk we could not understand him. By speaking English the lion would create the illusion of speaking our language, yet all the time he would be speaking lion and nothing but lion. Whatever he said would reflect lion culture and be fully intelligible only in the lion's lair. The theologians at the Council of Trent for the most part talked academic talk, the talk of culture two, and they translated Luther into their own language. Erasmus talked humanistic or literary talk, the talk of culture three, and he did the same with Luther. When expressed in their most radical forms, the four cultures are incommensurable with one another. They are rivals. To embrace one is to shut out the others.

Yet paradoxically, at many points they meet and embrace. In a Renaissance madrigal the poetry (culture three) gives shape to the music (culture four). Some things seem to straddle two cultures—*Hamlet* can be read as literature, yet its fullest expression is in performance. The trivium of logic, rhetoric, and dialectics was for a long time a basic component in the programs of both culture two and culture three. The cultures are rivals, yes, but they are also siblings. Their boundaries are permeable. No wall separates one of these Gulf Streams from the others, or from the ocean itself.

There is another paradox about the cultures. Each of them is binary. Each has two aspects or manifestations, which can seem to be in opposition to each other. One aspect is more contemplative, the other more active. The prophetic culture manifests itself in both monk and militant. In culture two, the academician coexists with doctors, lawyers, and others who actively apply technical information. The poet and the orator, that is, the poet and the statesman/politician, are generators of culture three and its product: the poet in touch with his own feelings and the orator in touch with the feelings and needs of others. (But the epic poetry of Homer and Virgil correlates well with the public-person ideal.) Culture four is the culture of both painters and performers.

I think it is possible to identify some individuals as almost unequivocally belonging to one culture and having little affinity with the others. Erasmus belongs uncompromisingly in culture three, and he comes about as close as humanly possible to being a "pure type." He showed little understanding of art or appreciation for it, he despised Scholastic learning (though he knew it better than he usually gets credit for), and he was shocked by Luther's plain talk. The Trent folk as a collectivity belong substantially in culture two, the Münster Anabaptists in culture one, along with individuals like Andreas Karlstadt and John Knox. I take it as axiomatic that the more fully individuals fit the definition of one culture the more intolerant they are of the other cultures or at least the more uncomprehending. In Italy I have met vacationing American academicians who looked at but did not see the works of art that surrounded them.

Relatively few people fit unambiguously into these categories. Some of the preachers in the Sistine Chapel during the Renaissance seemed equally adept at preaching in either the Scholastic or the humanistic style, a clue that they did not feel the incompatibility so obvious to Erasmus. Michelangelo belongs squarely in culture four, yet he wrote poetry of merit. Luther is one of the great prophetic figures in the history of the West, but he also pioneered changes in the mass that showed great sensitivity to its fourth-culture character.

The traditional "Father of Monasticism," St. Anthony the Abbot, belongs without qualification in culture one. Yet Benedictine monasticism, surely one of the most important Christian institutions in the Latin West, is not so easily categorized. Benedictines by definition renounce the world for the cloister, but in the cloister they center their lives on the liturgy, which they traditionally have enhanced with architecture and music of surpassing beauty. In the Middle Ages great abbots like those of Cluny, and even those of the austere Citeaux, knew their Cicero and Virgil. They governed, like the good public servants of culture three, and especially from the tenth to the thirteenth century assumed important leadership roles in society outside the monasteries. Monks have shown much less interest in the texts, approaches, and issues I identify with culture two, but the "Father of Scholasticism," St. Anselm, was a monk.

Thus most persons or phenomena manifest traits of all four cultures, but the question to be asked is, Which culture predominates? Better, Which culture structures the value system? What is the center and starting point of the individual or the institution that then gives shape to the configuration?

Some important phenomena in the history of Christianity display a remarkable malleability and have allowed themselves to be shaped by each of the four cultures in turn. Approaches to the Bible provide the best example. For Luther the Bible consisted essentially in "threats and promises," the basic pattern of discourse for culture one. For Scholastics like Aquinas it tended to be a database from which to draw ideas, whereas for culture three it was a book of spiritual inspiration and moral guidance. For artists it provided images expressive of profundities about human nature and its relationship to the divine.

Preaching, the first and fundamental Christian ministry, is another example. From the days of Origen in the late second century until the death of St. Bernard in the middle of the twelfth, preaching was directly or indirectly governed by the principles of grammar and rhetoric of culture three. The "homily," the dominant form for this period, was essentially an adaptation of the exegetical techniques of the classical *grammaticus,* a commentary on the text that followed it almost word by word.

With the advent of Scholasticism, theory about preaching, now explicitly propounded and elaborated upon in the *Artes praedicandi,* moved to a large extent into culture two and made it into an exercise in understanding and proving a point. In the late Middle Ages when more and more preachers began to denounce the corruption of the church or the corrupt morals of society at large, preaching on a popular level took on characteristics of culture one.

Virtually all the preaching I have mentioned so far took place outside mass. In the papal curia and a few other locations the ancient tradition survived during the Middle Ages and Renaissance of preaching during mass right after the reading or chanting of the gospel passage for the day. In such cases preaching becomes part of the liturgical action, so that it must to some extent conform to culture four.

Cultures?

Before proceeding further I should be a little clearer about what I mean by that much-abused word *culture.* I intend it in its common-sense meaning, as when we speak of, say, Italian culture as distinct from American culture. In such a case we might be most immediately mindful of seemingly superficial differences in ways of looking at things, but we sense that a deeper difference in life-values is what underlies them. It is not an accident, for instance, that in even the humblest *trattoria* in Italy the meal is served with impeccable courtesy and grace.

I am tempted to let the matter rest at that. I notice that C. P. Snow in his book on "two cultures" never really defined what he meant by culture, and he got away with it. (Well, he did not altogether get away with it once the critics went to work.) He was content to speak in passing of traits, prejudices, and assumptions. I will try to do a little better by elaborating on the description I gave above. I do not aim, however, at using the word with the precision of an anthropologist or a sociologist.

By culture I understand a configuration. The elements within the configuration are forms, symbols, institutions, patterns of feeling, patterns of behavior, and the like. Among such elements in culture two, for instance, are lectures, examinations, academic gowns, and, most certainly, the diploma. Style of discourse is an especially important element in the configuration of any given culture, constitutive and revelatory of its design. Professors talk differently from poets. When taken together, the elements express a set of reciprocally dependent values and interpretations of reality. The artist has different priorities than the prophet. The different priorities suggest how the internal logic of the configuration makes it self-validating to those living within it and resistant to other such configurations. Prophets sound unrealistic, even dangerously reckless, to the statesman. I use the word *configuration* because it indicates relationships and proportions. Values central to one culture may be found in another but not so centrally as to give it shape.

I have considered other words to capture what I am about—*traditions, styles, types, mind-sets, models, archetypes, paradigms,* and *value systems.* The last named has the advantage of indicating the core whence springs the internal coherence of my four realities, but it seems detached from their historical grounding. *Types, models, mind-sets, archetypes,* and *paradigms* have the same disadvantage, besides being just as overworked and pretentious as *cultures. Traditions* seems too flaccid. I see *style* as crucial to understanding them, as I hope to make clear, but in and of itself it does not convey the full sweep of what I intend. I will use all these words, but for better or worse, I settled on *cultures* for the primary designation.

I will pay special attention to styles of discourse because in ancient Athens cultures two and three confronted each other explicitly over this issue, and they did so again much more pointedly and protractedly in the sixteenth century. But I also pay attention to styles because they reveal, I believe, the genius of each culture and make the distinctions among them more palpable. In other words, I am writing more about *form* than about content. The two interact, of course, but insofar as the book deals more with *how* Luther spoke than with what he said, it differs from most other books that likewise indulge in a grand sweep of centuries. This is not an essay on the history of ideas, much less on the history of doctrine.

Style, sometimes misunderstood as merely an ornament of speech, an outer garment enclosing the thought, is in reality the ultimate expression of meaning. This is obviously true for poetry and great novels but just as true for the kind of texts with which we are dealing. If we are to get at the deep reality of those texts, we must recognize their styles as constitutive of them. That is a basic premise on which I base this book. For the cultures, as for individuals, style is the manifestation of their personalities. The French got it right: *Le style, c'est l'homme même.* Style *is* the man/woman. How I am—mean or kind, manipulative or straightforward—tells you the kind of human being I am. Style is, moreover, the artist. We regard Michelangelo as a great artist not because of *what* he painted or sculpted, usually conventional subjects, but because of *how* he painted or sculpted those subjects—because of his style.

If the book is about style, it is therefore about rhetoric. Here I understand rhetoric to mean any effective style of communication, so that even culture four might be said to have a rhetoric. The word is often used that loosely. In this generalized sense Luther was an effective rhetorician, as was, in an entirely different way, Thomas Aquinas. The word is of course often used disparagingly, "mere rhetoric," to mean insincere or vapid talk, a slur that has dogged it since the days of Socrates.

I will sometimes use rhetoric in its generalized sense but never in its disparaging sense. I will most often use it in its precise historical sense to mean the art of persuasion or, even more precisely, the art of oratory that traditionally was considered the culminating point of culture three. Although it is today rarely taught as such, it was a highly developed and sophisticated discipline. It was a subject that had norms and rules and principles, a subject that could be taught in school. It could be codified in textbooks, as with the pseudo-Ciceronian *Rhetorica ad Herennium,* Quintilian's *Institutiones,* and the countless successors to such classics through the centuries. Closely related to dialectics, the traditional discipline of culture two, it differed from it as the art of winning consensus differs from the art of winning an argument. Each of these arts expresses and engenders styles of discourse that are related but significantly different. Each thus expresses and engenders significantly different styles of thinking and evaluating—what I call culture two (dialectics) and culture three (rhetoric).

I imagine the relationships among the four cultures in the form of a cylinder. Down the length of the cylinder I would list in parallel columns the names that best typify a given culture at different moments in the history of the West—Tertullian, Gregory VII, Luther, and so on, for culture one; then for culture two Aristotle, Boethius, and so forth. By moving my eye down the length of the columns I remind myself of the distinctiveness of the cultures and of the historical continuity within them. I am reminded of their sometimes isolation from their neighbors alongside them and even of their occasional hostility to them. If I run my eyes around the cylinder horizontally or even walk around it keeping my eyes at the same level, I see how the cultures are neighbors to one another, almost touch one another. They almost hold hands. In the cylinder the icon of culture four finds itself side-by-side with culture one. Graven image though the icon is, in its ineffability it powerfully expresses the transcendence that is so much a concern of culture one. The cultures meld into one another.

They took shape, after all, in the same Mediterranean matrix and lived there for centuries before expanding into northern Europe and, eventually, across the seas. Jerusalem knew Athens long before the time of the New Testament and had spiritual and intellectual commerce with her. Tertullian, the great naysayer to Athens, was a product of Hellenistic civilization, an identity he could not possibly shake. Paul wrote in Greek, not Hebrew.

Even though in my cylinder the cultures appear in parallel columns, they are not perfectly parallel realities. I treat culture, therefore, as an analogous concept, verified somewhat differently in each of the analogues. Culture four differs from the others in not using words and in thus being an easy prey for the others, sometimes seeming to be not much more than a mode of the others. Culture one is otherworldly, but no matter how otherworldly prophets might hope to be, they must live in the time and place of this world. Even the Amish and cloistered nuns reveal in their clothing and other ways the situation of their founding. When the prophetic culture in cases like these assumes an institutional form, it loses some of its edge and experiences a certain dissipation. Cultures two and three, on the contrary, came to their most effective epiphany and densest expressions in their institutional forms—the university and the humanistic secondary schools.

Culture one also differs from the others in that it is more discontinuous within itself. Continuity is of course not altogether absent, especially after Luther provided such a striking model for the prophet-reformer. It is not an accident that Martin Luther King, Jr., bore the name he did. But by definition this culture best manifests itself in brilliant flashes, in an intensity that cannot be maintained. The other three cultures have a continuous history, but culture one is almost by definition episodic. It is staccato, the others legato. This difference is reflected below in that I make no attempt to treat culture one as a narrative, as if one prophetic moment followed with some logic upon another. I skip from one prophet to another.

Even for the other cultures I use narrative principally to illustrate the character of the culture in question and to set the stage for particular expressions of it. In these cultures, too, I skip and choose, sometimes arbitrarily, and I blithely ignore major figures and phenomena. I provide a sampling of profiles or sometimes not much more than a series of snapshots. Although I describe a few landmarks in their historical development, I am not attempting to write the history of the cultures. I am interested in recurring patterns and their interrelationships.

The word *patterns* suggests abstractions. Though I might seem to treat the cultures abstractly, they achieve reality only through the human beings who prophesy, prove, persuade, and love to parade. Sometime in their lives most human beings, we might assume, feel called upon or compelled to engage in every one of these activities. Consistency in engagement with one or the other of the activities is what produces the social phenomenon called culture. No culture without human agents. The four cultures are grounded in human beings, with their likes and dislikes, their fears and hopes—with their mothers and their fathers and their styles of upbringing.

Many of us seem to live in all four cultures at once, though one of them probably predominates over the others. But in that regard I am not even sure about myself, though I spend most of my waking hours in culture two. Some friends tell me I belong in culture three. I have on rare occasions participated in demonstrations and, shouting slogans, marched for causes I believed just. I perform liturgies, culture four, and I am deeply affected by them. Beyond liturgies I sometimes flee into that culture of beauty, dance, and play, and I find myself much at home there, satisfied. Affinities exist among the cultures because part of their reality is the reality of human temperaments and personalities. Temperaments and personalities do not admit of easy containment.

I get a better understanding of the four cultures, finally, by relating them, as already suggested, to those four great abstractions that medieval philosophers called the transcendentals: unity *(unum),* truth *(verum),* goodness *(bonum),* and beauty *(pulchrum).* I must admit stretching a bit to relate the first to the *unum,* but *unum* does suggest the horror of contamination by "the other" that drives culture one and suggests as well the integrity that is the central concern of that culture. The remaining transcendentals fit more neatly. Culture two is about truth. The creed of culture three channels energies either into action for the good of society or, in poetry, novels, and drama, into tending to the life we live. Culture four—beauty.

An Invitational Rhetoric

I must now answer a crucial question. If this book is about form, what is the form of the book? The most appropriate form, if objectivity is the primary value, would be one that is independent of the four forms with which it is concerned. But that is not possible. The book must stand in one of the cultures.

It is not a dance, concert, or painting, so culture four is excluded. I rule out culture one as patently inappropriate. Simply by assigning numbers to the cultures I might seem to favor the style of discourse of culture two, where, as I said, I spend most of my waking hours. I like to think the book is based on those culture-two hours. But I have cast it not in the form of that culture but in the form of culture three.

In its classical modality culture three has an endemic "weakness for general ideas." You can hardly imagine ideas more general than the four cultures. That is the first clue to the culture in which the book stands. Culture three in its poetic dimension, furthermore, is happy with the ambiguity that allows a text to be read at several levels at once. In a modest way I think my essay can similarly be read, as, for instance, a way of looking at the sixteenth-century conflicts and as a way of looking at some contemporary issues—as a way, moreover, of looking at oneself. And, unlike culture two, culture three is appreciative of meanderings, asides, and loose ends—appreciative of what one does in an essay.

I can be more specific within culture three. In a loose way I have tried to adapt from the tradition of culture three the classical genre of the epideictic, a fancy word that indicates the "art of praise and blame." It is the art of "ceremonial" rhetoric, which leads not to action or decision but to appreciation and contemplation. It is in frequent use even today in commemorating important causes, events, anniversaries, or persons. We experience it in commencement addresses, speeches at ribbon-cutting events, eulogies at memorial services. We experience it in jingoistic political speeches.

Lincoln's Gettysburg Address is an example of the epideictic genre at its best. In that speech Lincoln did not try to prove the war was just or to move his hearers to any action. He tried simply to raise appreciation for what was at stake and, at least by implication, to praise it as noble and worthy of the great cost. The mode of the genre, then, is not command or demonstration but invitation—an invitation to consider and to notice.

If small can be compared to great, I am aiming at something similar in this book. I am trying to set the cultures on the stage before your eyes. I want to hold them up for you to see so that you might admire them in all their brilliant plumage but also, in perhaps a more limited way, so that you see their neuroses and vanities. Through this genre I invite you to look at the cultures and consider them. I invite you to be generous with them, but at the same time I warn you not to let any one of them suborn you into thinking it is the whole show, which is what they like to do.

CULTURE ONE

Prophecy and Reform

THIS IS THE culture of contempt of the world. It expresses its contempt by withdrawing from worldly concerns. It expresses it also by words leading to action in the world. This culture is particularly contemptuous of sweet talk and artifice of speech. The uncompromising antitheses that the culture poses and that constitute its core manifest themselves in styles of discourse that tend to be equally uncompromising and themselves bristling with antitheses.

In the tradition of classical rhetoric (in Athens, therefore), public discourse was generally conceived as having the threefold function of teaching, pleasing, and persuading, with now one, now the other predominating according to the situation and genre. The prophetic tradition rejects this triad in favor of proclamation. The simplicity of the proclaimed message lends itself to expression in sound bite—"Support our troops."

Although all that prophets can do is cry out the truth, they can convey through the use of paradox something of the transcendence of the message and its inscrutable mystery. Paradox simultaneously affirms two seemingly incompatible things. Luther was a master of this device, as in *simul justus et peccator*—"at one and the same time sinner and justified." The paradox sometimes inverts values, "The last shall be first, the first last."

But paradox and its cousin oxymoron are rhetorical figures discussed in classical treatises on oratory. Prophets might disdain rhetoric, but they must speak in human words and patterns, which, when effective, are what we know as rhetoric. This reality points again to the inconsistency inseparable from denying Athens a place in Jerusalem. The prophetic culture, despite its professed straightforwardness, is the most elusive of the four.

Some Prophets and a Few Prophetesses

Tertullian (c.160–c.225), prolific Christian apologist and "the Father of Latin Theology," not only set the question that guides this book but also gave the typically prophetic answer to it. With exquisite irony he laid bare the pretensions of those who sneered at his faith: "The fault of the divine doctrine, I suppose, lies in its springing from Judaea rather than from Rome."[1]

In speaking of Christ's resurrection from the tomb, he affirmed it fell within the field of belief because it was silly or absurd or unbelievable *(ineptum),* pointing to the inscrutability of the revealed message and its imperviousness to the workings of the human mind: "And the Son of God died; it is by all means to be believed, because it is absurd. And he was buried and rose again; the fact is certain, because it is impossible."[2]

Tertullian loved to quote Paul to the effect that God chose the foolish of this world to confound the wise. He ended his days, moreover, as a Montanist, a member of the rigorously ascetical movement that condemned mainline Christians for their lax discipline and morals, for their compromises with the ways of the world. He would seem to belong squarely in the prophetic culture.

It is easy to justify placing Tertullian there, partly for what he actually believed and practiced and partly for the impact his words produced—for how he sounded and how he was often uncritically interpreted. But he belongs there with the heavy qualifications that weigh upon so many prophets. Tertullian was a product of both the philosophical and the rhetorical culture of his times. He knew the classical philosophers perhaps better than any early Christian thinker. True, he expressed a Christian opposition to "the world" in particularly strong and striking fashion and held views on the subject that were extreme, but he neither could nor wanted to renounce utterly what Greek and Roman culture had achieved. On one level he categorically denied that Athens had anything to do with Jerusalem, but on another, even sometimes explicit, level he admitted that it had much to do with it.

His question about Athens and Jerusalem can be seen as but an echo and reformulation of Paul's series of questions to the Corinthians, which Tertullian quotes again and again: "What partnership have righteousness and iniquity? Or what fellowship has light with darkness? What accord has Christ with Belial? Or what has a believer in common with an unbeliever? What agreement has the temple of God with idols?"

When Tertullian lets fly his vitriol against the philosophers, he does so because, despite the elements of truth they contain, they fall short of the fullness of truth that Christ brought. It is not right to stay with the imperfect when the perfect has arrived. The imperfect then becomes a perversion, even though before that moment it could act as a pointer toward the perfect. Many Christian writers of the early centuries argued in this fashion. What is special about Tertullian is that he made his case with almost unparalleled skill, which again points to how impressively he, like almost all Christian writers of the first millennium, can stand as an expression of culture three as much as culture one.

Nonetheless, for Tertullian, now that the perfect has come, Athens has lost its usefulness, at least for the most part. With such a stance he is perhaps living on one level and arguing on another, but it is with his argument that we are concerned. As with Augustine and Luther after him, his experience of being delivered from sin to grace profoundly affected his every statement. Until baptism he could not break the pattern of fornications that held him bound. He thus, like Augustine and Luther, saw the soul as corrupt, infected with Adam's sin, incapable on its own of good yet delivered unto good by grace alone. Here lies the psychological basis for the antithetical pattern of argument—sin/grace, corruption/goodness, with no room for anything in between.

Tertullian was an adult convert to Christianity, a small and despised sect. He joined this sect in large part because he believed Christians lived lives morally superior to those of pagans, and he found this belief confirmed in his own new moral strength upon baptism. He had become part of the chaste bride of Christ who stood as a reproach and challenge to the corruption in the society he had known and been part of. As the years passed, however, he discovered that Christians, too, committed fornication, adultery, murder, and even apostatized from their faith under the pressure of persecution. Worse than that, bishops in the church were offering ecclesiastical forgiveness to these sinners if they repented. He thus came to believe, like so many prophets, that he was living in especially perverse times, a sign that the world would soon end: "As evil more and more prevails—and this is a characteristic of the latter days—good is no longer permitted to be born, so corrupt is the race."[3]

He thus became a Montanist, a member of a minority movement within a minority religion. Mainstream consensus was for him almost by definition a sign pointing in the wrong direction: "As if one were not in greater danger of going astray with the many, since truth is loved in company with the few."[4]

It was principally the reality of a sordid church that precipitated Tertullian's move into Montanism, bringing with it a severe stance on ecclesiastical forgiveness. In embracing Montanism he was aware of a conversion in himself, of a radical change of course in his thinking on mercy, of now "opposing an opinion that I formerly held while in the company of the Sensualists."[5]

The Montanist prophetesses and ecstatics believed, moreover, that the special guidance of the Paraclete led them into truths not clear in the Scriptures, not clear to their fellow Christians: "The Paraclete, the Holy Spirit, whom the Father will send in my name, will teach you all things" (John 14.26). The guidance of the Paraclete provided Tertullian with warrant to stand against the bishops as they compromised the purity of the church and thereby failed to reflect God's avenging justice. Unless God will in the end set things right and balance the evil of the age, he cannot truly be God. As a prophet Tertullian must promise that in the end justice will prevail.

Justice, the word that appears so often in the discourse of the prophet, no matter how it is understood, thus emerges as a key to Tertullian's ever more rigorous disciplinary stance. This brilliant apologist for Christianity finally ended up interpreting the parable of the prodigal son, the parable of God's forgiveness, as applying to the repentant pagan but not to the repentant Christian. The church could never allow the apostate or the adulterer to reenter its portals. For him the law against adultery in the Old Testament became simply more severe with the New.

Tertullian was not a church reformer in the strict sense of someone with a program to correct, in a structural way, problems affecting ecclesiastical life. He lived long before the idea had been conceived that concerted efforts could rightly be expended in such a cause. Yet as authentic prophet he detested the soiling of the sacred and decried it. It is significant that he saw the cause of the corruption of the church to be *mediocritas,* that is, tepidity, standing midway between good and evil. Moral choices were clear and simple. The world was governed by the strife of opposites—of light with darkness and of good with evil.

Simplicity was for Tertullian the hallmark of truth. There was no need for subtleties, distinctions, dialectics, and inquiry: "Unhappy Aristotle! who invented dialectics, the art of building up and pulling down; an art so evasive in its propositions, so far-fetched in its conjectures, so harsh in its arguments, so productive of contentions—embarrassing even to itself, retracting everything and really treating of nothing!"[6]

Tertullian's lust for simplicity persists throughout his writings and was for him a hermeneutical principle. Not surprisingly, it had repercussions for his style: it helped generate his love for superlatives. Luther, known to his enemies as the *doctor hyperbolicus,* had the same propensities, but Tertullian anticipated him. "Indignation," he said, "forces us to speak."[7] Indignation usually erupts into exaggeration.

The simplicity Tertullian so highly prized also helped generate his penchant for paradoxes, to which his Stoic background already inclined him. The New Testament, where in the gospels the first being last and the last being first was a leit-motif, provided precedent. Tertullian accepted paradox as a means of putting forth truth's simplicities and of stating them without fussy qualifications. The simultaneous affirmation of two seemingly contrary ideas is of a pattern with the stark disjunctions and radical antitheses that also mark his style. What paradox says is that truth is to be found not in the middle but at both ends.

Tertullian argues with his opponents and tries to persuade them to his point of view, but in theory he disdains both dialectic and rhetoric. Extraordinarily skilled in the art of sarcasm, invective, and ridicule, which even today gives naughty delight to those who read him, he in the end used his art as the herald of the often unpleasant truths that he knew himself to be.

In witness, especially the witness of martyrdom, the prophetic message expresses itself more powerfully than in words. Tertullian is possibly the editor of the account of the martyrdom in 203 of Saints Perpetua and Felicity during the persecution of the emperor Septimius Severus. Perpetua was a young married woman of Carthage and Felicity her slave, both catechumens. The account, couched largely in the women's own words, helped make this martyrdom especially well known in the Christian community, which very early began to celebrate the anniversary. It also very much influenced later accounts of Christian martyrdom and helped promote it as an ideal: to suffer and die for Christ as he suffered and died for us. Martyrdom would be a recurrent and powerful theme in prophetic culture.

Saint Catherine of Alexandria, if she ever lived, would have been martyred about a century after Perpetua and Felicity. According to the legend, which originated at Mount Sinai in the ninth century, Catherine, of royal birth, rejected the emperor's proposal of marriage, successfully defended Christianity in disputation with fifty philosophers, and protested with the emperor against the persecution of Christians. In the Middle Ages and Renaissance Catherine was one of the most popular saints. In England alone sixty-two churches were dedicated to her, and she appears prominently in countless paintings. She was the patron of young girls, of spinners and weavers, of students, and especially of philosophers, which means her feast was celebrated with special solemnity in the Arts faculty of medieval universities. The *Golden Legend,* the thirteenth-century compilation that became the standard source for lives of the saints, quotes her words to Emperor Maxentius: "I am Catherine, only daughter of King Costus. Though born to the purple and quite well instructed in the liberal disciplines, I have turned my back on all that and taken refuge in the Lord Jesus Christ. But the gods you worship can help neither you nor anybody else. O unhappy devotees of idols that when called upon in need are not there, who offer no succor in tribulation, no defense in danger!"[8] For her bold speech and her steadfastness in her beliefs, she was tortured on the wheel and then beheaded.

But the persecutions ceased shortly after Catherine's martyrdom, and another equally powerful ideal arose. In that century St. Athanasius, bishop of Alexandria and archenemy of the Arian heretics, wrote a life of St. Anthony of Egypt (251–356). The book was an immediate success, the first great classic of Christian hagiography and a best-seller into the modern era. In the *Confessions* Augustine related how, just before his conversion, he heard from his friends about Anthony and about how just reading the book filled Christians with love of holiness. In the Italian Renaissance Anthony appears in numerous paintings, often with founders of religious orders like Francis and Dominic—his popularity due ultimately to the book Athanasius (or somebody from Athanasius's circle) wrote about him. As Jean Leclercq said of Anthony, "He remained truly the Father of all monks, and so in all milieus and in every period of the Western Middle Ages they considered themselves as truly his sons. Everywhere they claimed his support, sometimes even against each other."[9]

How much Athanasius, bishop and person of the establishment, tamed this famous hermit and holy man for his own purposes is an open question. In this telling, the ordered discipline of Anthony's life contrasts with the eccentricities and unpredictability of other solitaries who were his contemporaries. No matter, it was Athanasius's portrait of Anthony that had the impact and provided the prototype for prophets whose loudest word about Athens would be the contempt they expressed for it by their withdrawal into desert places. Certain features of Athanasius's Anthony henceforth would constitute the essential profile of men and women whose lives were animated by *contemptus mundi.*

Born of devout and reasonably prosperous Christian parents, according to Athanasius, Anthony as a boy "could not bear to learn letters" and after his conversion to holiness as a young adult was "taught by God."[10] His conversion occurred when he heard the words from Matthew's gospel, "If you would be perfect, go, sell what you possess and give it to the poor, and you will have treasure in heaven." He did just that and withdrew into the desert at Pispir in Egypt, where his solitude was from time to time interrupted in three different ways: first by his successful conflicts with the demons who attacked and tempted him; second, by men of letters and smooth talk as well as by dialecticians, who, considering themselves wise, came to ridicule him (in this contest of words and wits Anthony showed them to be the true fools); and third, by disciples and would-be disciples who wanted to hear his wisdom. For this last group he even emerged from his solitude for a while to organize them, loosely, into a community. Although Anthony had not so far as we know studied the writings of the Arians, he knew they were wrong.

What do we have here? First, a conversion. Then an ignorance superior to all secular learning. Anthony is a man of one book, the Bible. Despite his withdrawal into solitude, conflict of one kind or another defines his situation. Most important, the radical action of fleeing from the world as far as possible defines his person.

But in this last point lies, according to Anthony and the other Fathers of the Desert, the deepest paradox and irony: it was not they but their critics who were truly in flight, for by indulging in the things of this world they fled from themselves. These worldlings were the truly alone, destitute of comfort and peace, alienated from their very souls. Anthony's withdrawal, on the contrary, was not only not flight; it was harkening to a call to arms.

Anthony, the wrestler with demons, emerges from Athanasius's pages with a certain humanity and some common sense, which help account for the book's success through the centuries with persons following a wide variety of lifestyles. Intent though Anthony is on his goals and uncompromising with the demons, he is flexible in his relations with those who seek him out. This quality is also reflected in many of the "Sayings" of the Desert Fathers that through Cassian and others were transmitted to the West.

But in others the rejection of this world could take the form of in-your-face extremes. St. Simeon (c.390–459) was the first of the Stylite or pillar ascetics. He and his many imitators of course renounced marriage and engaged in severe fasting and other bodily austerities. But most remarkable was the fact that they lived out their days atop pillars, exposed to all the elements and in some cases with not enough room to lie down. The rich hagiographical literature about them presents them admiringly as spiritual athletes and saintly champions who fought off all the attacks and seductions of the demons. They lived in a world peopled by the good and the bad, where life-choices were clear-cut. St. Daniel the Stylite (409–493) dealt with his disciples the way the other saints dealt with theirs: "he led their hearts away from soul-destroying questioning and kept them unshaken in the faith."[11]

The withdrawal of these austere figures from human society was a variation on the rich biblical themes of wilderness and desert that would continue to play themselves out in a multitude of ways through the centuries into the modern era. The desert, the wilderness, is a place of strife/peace, of demons/angels, of primordial chaos/paradise, of purgatory/utopia.

For palpable impact on Western sensibilities among those who hold the world in contempt, Anthony and the stylites pale alongside John the Baptist and Mary Magdalene. If portraits of Anthony were popular in art from the Middle Ages forward, the number of portraits of the Baptist and the Magdalene were incomparably more so.

John withdrew to the desert, took as food only honey and locusts, dressed in a scant garment of camel's hair—artists would depict him almost nude. He preached repentance and conversion, and he proclaimed Jesus' true identity. He denounced Herod's sin and was put to death for it—a prophet indeed, for he was a martyr for the truth. The baptistry of the Lateran basilica in Rome, with his statue on the edge of the baptismal pool, was consecrated in his honor during the reign of Constantine himself, and his cult grew only more important through the Middle Ages. He is the patron saint of many European cities, including Florence.

John was an inspiration for the charismatic preachers who began to appear in the West in the eleventh and twelfth centuries, among them Henry of Lausanne, who after a period of withdrawal as a hermit took it upon himself to denounce the worldliness and wealth of the clergy in France and Italy. Not ordained himself but intent on clerical rectitude, he preached, like others before and since, that the validity of the sacraments depended on the worthiness of the minister. An even more famous recluse who made his name as a preacher was Peter the Hermit. During the First Crusade with the cry "God wills it," he inspired thousands of Christians to defy worldly wisdom by abandoning their homes to join the band he led across Europe. The result was tragic for them as well as for almost everybody who crossed their marauding and sometimes murdering path.

Mary Magdalene had early on in the Western tradition been conflated with Mary of Bethany (John 12) and the sinful woman in chapter seven of Luke. Soon the legends of her years of penance, spent withdrawn in a cave in Palestine after Jesus' ascension or, later, in a cave in Provence, were in circulation. In the *Golden Legend* she has one of the longest entries and is depicted after her putative arrival in Marseilles as a powerful preacher of the Christian message, woman though she was. Shaking with anger on one occasion, she upbraided the governor of the province for not helping poor Christians: "Why, when you are so rich, do you allow the saints of God to die of hunger and cold? . . . you sleep, tyrant, limb of your father Satan, with your viper of a wife . . . you enemy of the cross of Christ . . . Wicked man, you will not escape or go unpunished."[12] Her iconography consists essentially in the long blond hair that covers her penitential nakedness.

By the fifteenth century in Italy St. Jerome began to appear in altarpieces and other paintings almost as often as did the Baptist and Magdalene. Preachers delighted in the story of his famous dream. Jerome loved the Latin classics, which of course had constituted the substance of his formal education. One night as he slept he saw himself appearing before the judgment seat of Christ. When upon interrogation he professed he was a Christian, the judge thundered back, "You lie. You are not a Christian but a disciple of Cicero," and he ordered him to be flogged. Jerome begged mercy and foreswore possessing or reading the classics ever again.

The dream made a deep impression upon him, but later in life he made accommodation with the classical culture that, even had he wanted to, he could not possibly have shed, since it was so much a part of him. But for preachers and reformers in subsequent centuries the story ended with the dream, with Cicero having nothing to do with Jerusalem.

In many paintings Jerome appears as scholar or cardinal, but he is just as often depicted as a gaunt ascetic, paired at times with John the Baptist. Like John he is often almost nude. The *Golden Legend* emphasizes this penitential and reclusive aspect of his life but also mentions his efforts to reform the clergy. His cult acquired a firm institutional base and received new impetus in the latter half of the fourteenth century, when in Spain and Italy five new monastic congregations bearing his name were founded to imitate the supposed lifestyle of this refugee from the world.

The renunciation by such ascetics thus included, within the limits of modesty, the renunciation of clothing. Stripped clean. Jerome laid the foundation for the powerful symbolism of this stripping. Quoting to Paulinus of Nola Christ's injunction to sell all one has, give it to the poor, and follow him, he exhorted Paulinus to do just that, "nude following the nude cross."[13] He returned to the idea in other places. In the itinerant preaching of the eleventh and twelfth centuries the idea took off and eventually achieved its axiomatic form, beloved of the Franciscans, "nude to follow the nude Christ"—*nudus nudum Christum sequi*—Christ stripped by the Roman soldiers, then nude on the cross. Giotto (or, more likely, pseudo-Giotto) immortalized the moment Francis of Assisi signaled total renunciation of his former life by stripping himself nude for all to see.

The axiom and the act catch the radical inversion of values, the paradox, endemic to prophetic culture. This nudity is alluring and handsome, yet counter-erotic, for to be thus nude is to be clothed in the most radiant garment, to have "put on Christ" (Rom.13.14). To be thus nude, bereft of covering even for one's loins, is to enjoy a wealth beyond all telling. It is to return to the naked innocence of Paradise, a nudity therefore without shame. It signifies the re-establishment of the harmony that "in the beginning" reigned in that wilderness, where all creation was bound together in friendship. The prophet's promise is fulfilled.

Primordial harmony meant friendship between humans and wild beasts. One evening a lion limped into Jerome's monastery retreat in Bethlehem. The monks fled in terror, but Jerome received him as a guest and tended his wounded paw. The lion, as the *Golden Legend* relates, "lost all his wildness, and lived among the monks like a house pet."[14] He was given the task of leading to pasture and defending the ass that carried the monks' firewood to them. The two animals became friends. Few are the portraits of Jerome in which he is not accompanied by that wonderful lion.

Many centuries later *The Little Flowers of St. Francis* related a similar story. Francis went out to confront the ravenous wolf that terrorized the town of Gubbio. As the beast approached, Francis made the sign of the cross over it: "Come to me, Brother Wolf. In the name of Christ I order you not to harm me or anyone." The wolf lowered its head and lay down at the saint's feet as if a lamb. Francis set forth the terms of a peace pact, which the wolf happily accepted. They then shook hands to seal their friendship, another moment immortalized in the fresco attributed to Giotto. From that day forward the wolf harmed no one. When he was hungry he was received with courtesy in Gubbio as he went from door to door, where he was always given his supper, and "it is a striking fact that not a single dog ever barked at him."[15]

Legends like this about Francis abound. He preached and the birds listened. The stories are too consistent to be altogether inconsistent with the historical person, but some, surely, are better grounded in fact than others. Francis had to undergo cauterization with a red-hot lancet for a chronic eye affliction. The brethren who accompanied him to the doctor withdrew, so as not to have to witness the brutal operation. "Brother Fire, more beautiful and useful than other things," said Francis, "be kind to me, for long have I loved thee in the Lord." After the operation he attested he had felt no pain. Thomas of Celano, his biographer, commented, "He had returned to the innocence of Paradise, and, if he chose, even the wild elements were tame before him."[16]

Pope Gregory VII

The Gregorian Reform, or the Investiture Controversy, is generally regarded as one of the great turning points in the history of the West. It initiated, for instance, a significant redefinition of how the papacy would function, sparking its development as more visible, vigilant, and centralized, more conscious than ever before of its preeminence over other bishoprics and even over earthly monarchs.

The phenomenon manifested itself in a complex series of events that in its more obvious phase stretched from the beginning of the pontificate of Leo IX in 1049 to the Concordat of Worms in 1122. Its most intense period was the pontificate of Gregory VII, 1073–1086. Gregory's conflict with Emperor Henry IV of Germany led to civil war in Germany, to the siege and sacking of Rome by imperial and Norman forces, and to the death of the pope in exile. Historians see it as the first massive "Church-State" clash in the history of Western Christianity, which set the pattern for further clashes to come. They have described it as the great frontal attack on feudalism, as a challenge to the principles out of which society had operated more or less since the collapse of the Roman Empire in the West. They are unanimously agreed on its importance, no matter from what perspective they analyze it. But in my opinion they rarely emphasize sufficiently how by word and deed "the Gregorians" provide the first striking example of the transformation of the traditional idea of reform, which up to that time had mostly been applied to conversion in individuals or to local situations. The Gregorians, without being fully aware of it, applied reform to a system, to a large social reality.

As the Gregorians step-by-step came to formulate their aims into a program, they introduced into the West a startling new phenomenon: a relatively small and materially meager group could be marshaled to effect a profound change in the way certain institutions of society operated, a group ready to challenge the powerful who identified with those institutions. The Gregorians were not simply ascetics denouncing in the traditional way the sins and shortcomings of the social and political establishment; they challenged and wanted to replace the very assumptions the establishment (and the rest of society) took for granted. In the ultimate implications of their program, they sought not adjustments in a system but a new system.

Nothing with such systemic pretensions had been known or attempted before. True, the reformers finally had to settle for adjustments, but they introduced into Western history the idea of the legitimacy and sometimes necessity of across-the-board reform—in the church and in other institutions of society. Even though the idea would not be clearly enunciated until much later, most notably at the Council of Constance in the early fifteenth century, with its call for "reform in head and members, in faith and practice," the Gregorians opened the way for the change.

Gregory and others in the movement were deeply imbued with monastic ideals, and Peter Damian, one of the leaders who had been called out of his hermitage to work for the reform, yearned to return there. Gregory had great reverence for the Rule of St. Benedict. This helps explain how clerical celibacy became the first plank in the Gregorians' program. For them the celibacy of the clergy was a moral issue, sometimes with even mystical overtones, that reached back to the Fathers of the Desert.

But the new element that especially sparked the energy and zeal of the Gregorian movement was the recovery and renewed study of ecclesiastical legislation from earlier centuries. The combustion of the prophetic impulse ignited the otherwise inert collection of canons to produce the organized social aggression of the Gregorian Reform. The protagonists of the papal party, though their deepest impulses derived from traditional moral and ascetic concerns, tried to secure their position through a heavy reliance on ecclesiastical texts. They were in that regard the harbinger and partial cause of the "legal renaissance" of the twelfth century.

These documents enabled the Gregorians to see that in earlier and better times bishops were not appointed or invested in their office by secular rulers, as was done in their own day, but elected by local clergy. The legal texts helped them to see the discrepancy between the present and the presumably normative past. This was their eureka-experience.

Because of that enlightenment, they felt compelled to change the present to make it conform to the true standard. As Gregory explained to Anno, archbishop of Cologne, regarding clerical celibacy, "You know, my brother, that these orders are not of our own invention but that we proclaim them as decrees of the ancient fathers, taught to them by the inspiration of the Holy Spirit."[17]

Like all reform movements at least until the Enlightenment (and arguably even after it), this one was essentially backward-looking. In that sense it was conservative. But as Brian Tierney observed about Gregory and his entourage: "It is no very uncommon paradox in Western history that the literal application by would-be reformers of half-understood old texts from a different historical epoch can have revolutionary implications for their own times."[18] A literal and full implementation of the strictures against lay investiture that the Gregorians, especially an extremist like Cardinal Humbert of Silva Candida, sometimes demanded would have utterly turned society on its head—something no secular ruler intended to let happen. Surely nobody so imbued with ideas of theocratic kingship as Emperor Henry IV was going to let it happen. The conflict over how prelates are appointed and invested with their office was, ultimately, a question of who was in charge of the church.

The Gregorian Reform is larger than Gregory. It began before he became an important player in the drama, and it continued after his death. It nonetheless rightly bears his name. His clash with Henry over the investiture question compelled him to articulate the ideals of the movement in particularly sharp fashion. By force of his words, actions, position, and personality he towers above all the other larger-than-life personalities associated with the movement. He saw himself as a prophet—telling the truth, calling the powerful to account, pleading for justice in a just cause, ready to take the consequences. As he lay dying he paraphrased Psalm 45: "I have loved justice and hated iniquity, therefore I die in exile."

No one is neutral about Gregory—the hallmark of a prophet. His contemporaries came to the most divergent opinions about him. As Bishop Guy of Ferrara, who had observed Gregory up close, put it, "The Christian people was divided in two, some saying he was a good man but others calling him an impostor and one who lived at odds with what befits a monk and a Christian."[19] Peter Damian, friend in a sometimes tense friendship, called him at one point "my holy Satan."[20] There were many, sometimes contrasting, aspects to his personality.

He took a stand against the most powerful and prestigious ruler of his day. In their conflict Gregory believed, not unreasonably, that he did not pick the fight. He entered into it reluctantly, not least of all because of the great esteem in which he held the emperor's father, the exemplary Henry III, and the cordial relations he had up to that point enjoyed with members of the imperial family.

From the first days of his pontificate he nonetheless presented himself as a prophet. No sooner had he become pope than he wrote to his allies in Lombardy, a place already simmering and soon to boil over as a focal point in his conflict with Henry: "I desire you to know, beloved brethren, as many of you do know already, that we are so placed that, whether we will or no, we are bound to proclaim truth and justice to all peoples, especially to Christians, according to the word of the Lord: 'Cry aloud; spare not, lift up thy voice like a trumpet and declare unto my people their transgressions.'" He spoke out against wrong, as he says elsewhere, not because he wanted to but because "we are driven on by the word of the prophet Ezekiel upon peril of our ruin, 'If thou dost not speak to warn the wicked from his way, that wicked man shall die in his iniquity but his blood will I require at thine hand.'" He could not be the dumb dog afraid to bark. Toward the end, when Henry's armies were about to defeat him, he called for help from the "few indeed, who stand up and face the wicked even unto death."[21]

The proclamation, the loud cry, the trumpet, the bark of a dog—that is the prophet's sound. Gregory's letters, peremptory in tone, lay down clear alternatives—one good, one bad. He saw the church engaged in a great cosmic battle—the members of Christ's body at war with the members of Satan's. In such a great conflict neutrality was not possible. Prophetic rhetoric provokes a crisis situation. By definition given to confrontation, it forces decision.

Gregory the prophet does not argue his point or try to persuade anyone to it. Take it or leave it—but leave it at peril to your immortal soul. He validated his message by invoking a self-evident and irrefutable test for its authenticity, Scripture, which was more fundamental in his thinking than the legal texts but in his mind altogether consonant with them.

What, however, were the hermeneutical lenses through which he read Scripture, that complicated collection of texts? How did he make it serve his purposes? Like Luther after him, he, without saying so, saw Scripture as a book of "threats and promises." Threaten and promise is what prophets do. He also found in it a blueprint for world order. That blueprint indicated the proper apportionment of tasks in the world to ensure that justice might prevail and especially that the church would function freely, untrammeled by sin and by bondage to the members of the Anti-Christ.

Freedom! That was the reward at the end of the trial; it was the promise sure to be fulfilled. More specifically, bishops would be elected *freely,* for the good of the church, not for the good of some earthly kingdom or dukedom. The "liberty of the church" *(libertas ecclesiae),* a theme in Gregory's correspondence, encapsulated what he hoped to achieve especially in his contest with Henry, and it emerged as a slogan for what the Gregorians were all about. Slogans like his would become an important piece of rhetoric for subsequent reformers, functioning as cheer, loyalty test, battle cry, and even battle axe. "The liberty of the church" soon became an ecclesiastical commonplace, hauled out for duty ever since in church-state conflicts. Freedom would be achieved with the triumph of justice, of righteousness.

Gregory's style is almost devoid of irony, but his story is riddled with it. It is ironical that freedom and righteousness would also be the battle cry of Luther, whose program for reform was almost the antithesis of what the Gregorians worked for. It is ironical (and almost unique) that a prophet should arise from an institution, from an office of the establishment like the papacy. It is ironical that the cry for the reform of the church that the papacy introduced into

Western Christianity would in the sixteenth century be so virulently turned against it.

Luther and the Reformation

Calls for reform of the ecclesiastical system and especially of the papacy became increasingly insistent in the late Middle Ages, with the "spiritual" branch of the Franciscan order often the most strident and insistent voice in the growing clamor. The scandal of the Great Western Schism, when for some forty years two and then three individuals claimed to be the legitimate pope, helped provoke a sense of living in especially corrupt times. Preachers proclaimed the imminent and much-needed advent of an "angelic pope," while other Christians fretted about clerical concubinage and the simony rampant, it was said, in Rome. On the eve of the Reformation, Savonarola fulminated in Florence against corruption in church and society, which resulted in his execution.

Luther, especially with his "Appeal to the German Nobility" of 1520, gave voice and center to the pent-up frustrations. In so doing he unwittingly encouraged enthusiasts of various kinds much more radical than he, who got lumped together under the pejorative label Anabaptists. A sense of utter differentiation from the world marked all Anabaptists, but, as mentioned, some went so far as to take up the sword for the slaying of unbelievers. At Münster in 1535 that option led to a bloodbath when a military force supported by both Catholics and Lutherans destroyed the godly in their citadel.

The peaceable among the Anabaptists manifested their unworldliness, however, by refusing not only to participate in either the old or any of the new churches but also to perform what were regarded as essential civic duties. They refused to bear arms, to swear civic oaths, and to serve in civic office. They would form a community apart, continually purified by excommunication of the lapsed. It is not altogether surprising that the "Schleitheim Articles," 1527, the first important synodal statement of such principles, was drawn up by a former Benedictine monk, Michael Sattler.

As such Anabaptists clearly foresaw, their stance brought them persecution by Catholics and mainline Protestants alike. They were ready to bear it, without resisting. That stance, certainly not new in the history of Christianity, was a prototype of what in 1840 Thoreau would call civil disobedience—active or passive resistance to injustices enshrined in law. Despite the opprobrium and oppression these communities have suffered through the centuries, some have persevered down to the present. The Mennonites (or Amish) are the best known. The Quakers, though of later and different genesis, in certain basic ways resemble them. Their lives are their word—of challenge and of invitation.

But in the tradition of the West Luther is *the* reformer. The Protestant churches on the streets of the cities and towns of the Northern Hemisphere are monuments witnessing to his importance. "Here I stand. I can do no other"—every educated person knows to whom to attribute that line. His name is familiar to persons of the most modest schooling.

Luther, even more than Gregory, is a person of extraordinary complexity, as the sheer mass of the scholarship about him for the past hundred years shows. He is too big for categories. He is too big for the four cultures. He lived his life in universities, culture two. He appreciated the philological aspects of culture three and was not insensitive to other aspects. He wrote hymns, revised the musical settings for the liturgy, and distanced himself from the iconoclasm of other reformers—he was not alien to culture four.

Yet if there is one category that comes closest to capturing him it is, I believe, prophet. Philipp Melanchthon likened him to those glorious figures of the Old Covenant because he had as his mission the renewal of the church, the New Israel. Other contemporaries saw him as God's ambassador, the very definition of prophet. Theologian he also was, of course, but theologian whose prophetic mode created a style of discourse that set him apart from the theological mainstreams and rendered him almost unintelligible to them. For that reason Gerhard Ebeling correctly describes him as a "linguistic innovator" and even more tellingly as a "language-event."[22]

Luther was a reformer, yes, but not a reformer to tinker with the system. He was a reformer with a stance so prophetically radical that it put his life at stake. He made active protest against systemic wrongdoing an accessible and admirable ideal.

Luther's discovery of Paul's Gospel—"justification by faith alone"—was for him a dramatically reorienting insight, a eureka-experience, a conversion that led to a sharp and irreversible break with his past: "Here I felt that I was altogether born again and had entered paradise itself through open gates."[23] He saw things utterly differently from before, as he discovered the true meaning of the Epistle to the Romans. He soon became convinced that he saw them utterly differently from his contemporaries, who lived in blindness and bondage.

Reformers up to then, including the Gregorians, postulated a discontinuity in morals, discipline, and charismatic gifts between their times and earlier, better times. But Luther's great and frightful insight was that the discontinuity extended to doctrine. The most vital and essential function of the church, the preaching of the Good News, the preaching of the essential truth of Christianity, had been interrupted for long ages and had even been suppressed by the papal church. A hard truth, which the ecclesiastical and theological establishments could not and would not bear to hear. He stood alone—against the powers of darkness.

The drastic reforms of ministry, piety, and church order that Luther set in motion were corollaries of his insight into the true nature of *justitia,* righteousness. Yet viewed from another angle, they turn out to be a long-delayed backlash to what centuries earlier the Gregorians strove for in their quest for *justitia.* Fundamental to them was their exaltation of papal authority; Luther repudiated the papacy altogether. The Gregorians cited the ancient canons as warrant for their reforms; Luther hurled the book of canon law into the flames. The first plank in their program was clerical celibacy; Luther took Katherine Bora in matrimony. They aimed at reducing the role of secular rulers in ecclesiastical affairs; Luther called them in to reform the church. Much of what the Gregorians had hoped to achieve was by the sixteenth century at least normatively in place. Luther would work to overturn it.

The launching of this reform, even in its preliminary and less radical form, met with rejection. From the time of his interview with Cajetan in 1518 until his appearance before the emperor at Worms in 1521, Luther faced a number of situations that approximated a courtroom, as attempts were made actually to bring him to trial—and possible execution. In Luther's eyes not he but God's Word stood in the dock. Finally, in January 1521 Luther was the object of the most severe judgment the church could deliver. The bull of excommunication, long in preparation, took effect. By April of that year, Luther was publicly rejected by Emperor Charles V himself and declared by him an outlaw of the empire.

Great dichotomies marked Luther's thought—the unbridgeable chasm between Christian and non-Christian, between Gospel and Law, between faith and works. The language Luther created to express the dichotomies not only manifests many of the characteristics of prophetic culture already mentioned but finds its voice in open conflict with cultures two and three—with the academic establishment of the Scholastic theologians and with the "new" rhetorical/literary movement personified in the humanist Erasmus.

Righteousness or justification cannot be earned. Grace would not be grace unless freely given. It is a gift of God that needs only to be accepted by faith, also God's gift. This is the righteousness that makes one good in God's eyes. According to Luther, the Scholastic theologians taught Aristotle's doctrine of goodness, goodness achieved by human effort: by doing good acts a person acquired good habits, a person who cultivated good moral habits became a good, virtuous person. This is what "reason" teaches, which utterly contradicts the Good News of "justification by faith alone," found according to Luther in the Bible—Scripture alone. There is here no bridge between Athens and Jerusalem. Persons virtuous in the eyes of the world are not virtuous in the eyes of God, for they have acquired their goodness by their own striving. Things are not what they seem.

Scholasticism's assumption that "reason" and the Good News were on some level compatible led to a number of other errors and abominations, but most important, it engendered an intellectual style that was inappropriate for the transcendent character of the Good News. Luther thus had to reject the Scholastics' attempts to structure their truths into the comprehensive schema of the *summa,* as if the Gospel could be put into a human structure. The Scholastics could do this because they accepted Aristotle's metaphysical system of form and matter, act and potency—the universe was explainable. They could do it because they accepted Greek teachings on logic and dialectics and believed that the syllogism would yield truth about justification.

Whereas the Scholastics tried through definitions and distinctions, through ever greater refinement of concepts, to arrive at resolution among seemingly incompatible realities, Luther preferred paradox. He explicitly framed his theses for his "Heidelberg Disputation," 1518, as a set of "theological paradoxes." Those paradoxes were content to sustain contrary positions in antithetical disjunction. In justification the Christian emerges at one and the same time as righteous and sinner. The lion lies down with the lamb.

The *simul* of Luther's paradoxes is paratactic adhesive, not a metaphysical solvent. The antithetical character of his paradoxes indicates his keen consciousness of disjunction and discontinuity. It helps explain his antipathy to the harmonious vision of the universe implied by the best of the *summae.* Those *summae* in their complacent, academic serenity conveyed none of the strife that is the Christian's lot in a world in which for the most part the Devil holds sway. Luther by contrast described his writings as a "crude and disordered chaos."[24] The medium is the message.

Thus the crucial point here is not the doctrine but the way Luther spoke about it. Luther had been trained as a Scholastic. Because he used words his opponents used, they thought they understood him. But Luther was Wittgenstein's lion. If you do what you can to be a good Christian, you sin grievously. That to Luther's opponents sounded heretical, yes, but it also sounded utterly absurd.

The Christian alone has access to a truth that contradicts all that his senses and reason might tell him about salvation. "Although the works of human beings always seem attractive and good," he asserts in the Heidelberg Disputation in 1518, "they are nevertheless likely to be mortal sins."[25] The deceptiveness of appearances is the cornerstone of what Luther called the theology of the cross, which is folly to the world. There is no way to reason with this folly, which is what culture two attempts. There is no artifice that can persuade one to accept it, which is what culture three would try. All that is left for someone speaking in its favor is to declare it. That is the proper style of discourse for the liberating message that God loves us because he loves us, freely. He loves us independent of our works and strivings, even of our sins. We cannot buy that love with the coin of our efforts.

Like the great prophets of old, Luther pointed to the transcendence of God, to mystery. The fundamental sin of the Scholastics was that they tried to know too much. They thought that, while paying lip service to God's incomprehensibility, they could figure it out. "Reason" brings God down to the level of our minds. Faith accepts that he is ever beyond. "Works" put God under obligation. Grace lets God be God, free.

On one essential level Luther's clash with Erasmus and with what Erasmus represented was identical to his clash with the Scholastics. He attacked Erasmus foremost because in Luther's view Erasmus, like all papists, espoused a Pelagian, save-yourself doctrine of justification. It was for that doctrine that Luther in 1525 first denounced him. But the antipathy ran deeper—to a conflict of cultures.

In his "Diatribe on Free Will," Erasmus concluded with a compromise that he hoped would bring all parties in the great uproar into agreement: attribute virtually everything in justification to grace, just a little bit to free will. Erasmus at that point sincerely believed he was reflecting the teaching of the Scriptures, but his solution was also consonant with culture three in its search for a viable compromise, in its hope to bring peace to all parties by avoiding extremes.

The very title "Diatribe" indicates, as Marjory O'Rourke Boyle has shown, its self-consciously rhetorical form. But the vocabulary Erasmus used with full deliberation to frame his conclusion is also typical of the discourse of the rhetorical culture. Erasmus explicitly stated that in such matters he hated assertions, the apodictic pronouncements Luther seemed to be slamming around everywhere on every topic. Moreover, "in the investigation into truth, I do not think that paradoxical formulas like these, not too far removed from riddles, should be used." Most tellingly, "I favor moderation."[26]

In Luther's eyes Erasmus could not have spoken in more damning terms than these. The cultural *style* to which this self-presentation pointed was for Luther perhaps even worse than the Scholastics' approach. It was dainty. Luther, glorying as "a barbarian among the barbarians," let fly at it the full fury of his contempt.

Peace at any price—that's what Erasmus was really about. According to Luther it mattered little to Erasmus what anyone believed anywhere, so long as the peace of the world was undisturbed. Erasmus was in Luther's eyes a skeptic. If Erasmus' teaching on justification did not make him ungodly, his mealy-mouthed dislike of assertions certainly would: "Not to delight in assertions is not the mark of a Christian heart. Indeed, one must delight in assertions to be a Christian at all. . . . Take away assertions and you take away Christianity." The Holy Spirit, no skeptic, has written not doubts and opinions on our hearts but assertions, "more sure and certain than life itself and all experience." This meant asserting the truth on its own clear terms, without embellishment or hedging, without minimizing the radical choices with which it confronts us: "We neither accept nor approve [Erasmus'] moderate, middle way."[27]

Erasmus, much in keeping with culture three, saw from his study of Scripture that peace and concord were "the sum and substance" of Christianity. Luther saw "the whole sum of the New Testament" to be justification by faith. That truth, Luther reminded Erasmus, came to change the world, even though in the proclaiming of it "the whole world had not only to be thrown into strife and confusion, but actually to return to total chaos and be reduced to nothingness."[28] Peace was the Devil's potion to drug the faithful to unwary sleep. Whereas Erasmus saw the cross as the efficacious sign of the reconciliation of the whole universe with God and as the lodestone by which Christ would "draw everything to himself," Luther saw it as the sign of contradiction.

Erasmus, conventionally devout in his younger years, gradually evolved into a person ever more seriously concerned with reform of theology, piety, and ministry and committed to doing something about it. But we have no evidence of a dramatic conversion of any kind (just as we have none for Thomas Aquinas). Luther had, however, been spun around—in an instant, he thought. Spun around from the darkness and prison of falsehood to the light and freedom of truth.

None of the prophets we have considered up to this point explicitly addressed culture four. But Luther's calling Christians to greater inwardness, his new teaching on the sacraments, his reworking of the liturgy, and his repudiation of papal "superstitions" encouraged other Protestant reformers to attacks, physical and theoretical, on sacred images, to radical redefinitions of Christian worship, and to reworkings of the rituals to express the new definitions. Luther had unwittingly fired the first salvo in the great crisis over art and sacred performance that shook especially northern Europe in the sixteenth century. Karlstadt, Zwingli, and Calvin would fire the next rounds and then lead the campaign to purify the church of idolatry and "ceremonies."

Luther spent a few months in Rome in the winter of 1510–11—the High Renaissance when Bramante, Raphael, Michelangelo, and many others were at work in one of the world's great outbursts of artistic genius. As we infer from his subsequent silence, he had no eyes to see what was going on—not so much because he was a prophet in the making but because he was a product of university culture where there was not the slightest opening in the curriculum or in the ethos for aesthetic experience.

But Luther could not avoid the issue of paintings and sculptures that represented religious scenes, of vestments and sacred vessels, or even of music. As we shall see, he was far less radical than others regarding these issues and more sensitive. Karlstadt, Zwingli, and Knox, for instance, see the manifestations of culture four as defiling the purity of God's Word, and they are in this regard much more typical of culture one than Luther was.

The paintings, vestments, candles, sacred vessels, and the like, creatures of culture four, had no words with which to defend themselves against criticism and calls for their abolition. They were defenseless against the predations of culture one, but also against the predations, less aggressive, of cultures two and three. All they could do was be themselves and perform. If verbal defenses were needed, they would have to come from the other cultures.

Abolition and Civil Rights

In the early nineteenth century the abolition movement in the United States picked up steam. It was fueled by a general sense that all was not well in the nation founded on such high principles and seemingly made secure by its unlikely victories over such a strong adversary in the Revolution and then again in the War of 1812. After a period of bracing confidence and optimism, many Americans, especially Northerners, began to think that the times were slipping out of joint. The very emergence of political parties signaled ominous differences of opinion about the country's destiny. Drunkenness, prostitution, and other forms of public immorality seemed more prevalent than ever before.

Church attendance had declined. The grounding of the body politic in orthodox, especially Calvinist, Protestantism seemed to be weakening. By the early years of the century the impact of the Enlightenment was ever more broadly felt, manifesting itself in the emergence of Unitarianism, a radical challenge to traditional Calvinism.

These were just a few of the elements that generated concern. It was in this context that the Second Great Awakening arose in 1800–1830, helping to foster the moral earnestness out of which the abolition movement was born. The Awakening spawned large-scale revivalist preaching that not only turned people's attention to the problems affecting society but inspired individuals to do something about them. Society needed reform if the future was to fulfill the promise of the past and the nation be set aright.

Preachers like Lyman Beecher organized revival meetings, sponsored missionary activity to unchurched reaches of the North and West, and in New England led crusades of one kind or another against the Unitarians. They railed against alcohol, gambling, and dueling. They tried to improve Sabbath observance by promoting and trying to enforce blue laws. Perhaps their most important achievement was their encouragement of voluntary associations dedicated to civic or moral causes, such as the Home and Foreign Mission Society (1812), the American Bible Society (1816), the African Colonization Society (1817), and the American Temperance Society (1826).

What about slavery? It was ever more discussed and debated. Although the emergence of slavery as an issue cannot be understood apart from other issues, it was about to become central, as a diffuse antislavery sentiment slowly condensed into calls for abolition. Despite the resistance of the churches to some aspects of the Enlightenment, even they began to accept principles of freedom and human rights as almost self-evident and, indeed, as sanctified in the Declaration of Independence, the foundational document of the godly nation.

Some Southerners felt the discrepancy between slavery and the righteous order of society and so emancipated their slaves. The discrepancy appeared all the more pronounced to Americans living in the North and West, at a distance from where the "peculiar institution" grounded an economy and a whole way of life. By about 1830 in New England, New York, and west of the Appalachians sentiment in favor of emancipation—some form of *gradual* emancipation—was becoming more common and more insistent. Just how emancipation could ever be accomplished was, however, a question to which there were few practical answers.

William Lloyd Garrison had nothing to do with the Great Awakening, but that movement prepared the stage for him to step upon as reformer *à outrance.* Born in 1805 in Newburyport, Massachusetts, he received a meager formal education but as a boy took easily to newspaper work, which sharpened his verbal skills. He learned his eloquence on the job and acquired his learning on the run. He remained essentially a journalist or publicist all his life. When in 1829 he went to Baltimore to help Benjamin Lundy publish the *Genius of Emancipation,* his career as an abolitionist began. He soon returned to Boston, where he would remain for the most part for the rest of his life.

Garrison, too, had few practical answers to the slavery question, but he assumed the prophet's role of denouncing slavery as an insufferable moral evil. A pacifist, he inflamed the political atmosphere with his rhetoric. Most abolitionists regarded him as an extremist, a loose cannon who did more harm than good—"the Massachusetts madman." He lost credibility for the cause of abolition because of his espousal of other equally unpopular causes—prohibition, women's suffrage, radical reform of a corrupt clergy and corrupt churches. But even for abolitionists his most extreme and unrealistic demand was for *immediate* abolition—for emancipation complete and entire *now,* no matter what the consequences.

How this immediate emancipation was to be accomplished without bloodshed Garrison never made clear. He continued for three decades to express his opposition to war and to anything that looked like preparation for war, testifying loudly against the construction of naval ships, armories, fortifications of any kind, and against the establishment of standing armies. He never acknowledged that his words and actions contributed to a situation where war became almost inevitable.

Nor did he ever adequately explain how, when war finally broke out, he was able to give it his unstinting support. Until that moment he seems to have believed that in some mysterious way his preaching of emancipation and other causes would hasten the day when the kingdoms of this world would become the kingdom of God.

If abolition for whatever reason could not be accomplished by peaceful means, Garrison advocated the separation of the North from the sinful South. Flee defilement! For him disunion was certainly not a solution to the problem, but it was the only course consonant with his pacifism and with the urgency of insulation from the contamination of slavery. By this stance he managed to intertwine the cause of the Union with the cause of emancipation. In 1844, largely under Garrison's leadership, the American Anti-Slavery Society adopted as its rallying cry and its motto, "No union with slaveholders!" No compromise.

Few important figures in modern times more perfectly fit the profile of the prophet and better exemplify the style of prophetic discourse than does Garrison. Threats and promises—"Woe to this guilty land!. . . The blood of millions of her sons cries aloud for redress! IMMEDIATE EMANCIPATION can alone save her from the vengeance of Heaven, and cancel the debt of the ages."[29]

On January 1, 1831, he published in Boston the first number of *The Liberator,* and he did not bring the newspaper to rest until thirty-five years later, in 1865, after emancipation had been accomplished. Others wrote for the paper, but Garrison held the editorship tightly in his hands and used the paper to proclaim without surcease the truth for which he took up the pen. As with Gregory and Luther, the words *liberty* and *justice* recur as leitmotifs.

"I will be harsh as truth, and as uncompromising as justice," he announced in the first issue. "On this subject [of slavery] I do not wish to think, or speak, or write, with moderation. No! No! Tell the man whose house is on fire to give a moderate alarm, tell him moderately to rescue his wife from the hands of a ravisher . . . urge me not to use moderation in a cause like the present. I am in earnest—I will not equivocate—I will not excuse—I will not retreat a single inch—AND I WILL BE HEARD."[30]

Garrison took opposition as a sign of the justice of his cause, as that same editorial made clear: "Opposition, and abuse, and slander, and prejudice, and judicial tyranny are like oil to the flame of my zeal. I am not dismayed; but bolder and more confident than ever. . . . I will not hold my peace on the subject of African oppression. If need be, who would not die a martyr to such a cause?"[31] From this point forward he returned often and fondly to the theme of his possible martyrdom.

Garrison was active that same year of 1831 in organizing the New England Anti-Slavery Society and two years later the American Anti-Slavery Society. The latter soon split into two factions—Garrison and his "extremism" against those who opposed him. At a tumultuous meeting in New York in 1840 the two factions collided in a battle that ended in formal schism. At the meeting Garrison rode high on only a thin margin of votes, but afterward his policies emerged as more or less the official policies of the society. He retained the presidency until the dissolution of the society in 1865. The "gradualists" and other anti-Garrison forces separated and founded a new body, the American and Foreign Anti-Slavery Society.

Despite some successes like these, Garrison was convinced that his was a lonely voice in the country at large, and in that persuasion he was for the most part correct. His sense of standing almost alone only increased his sense of mission: "The whole nation is against me. . . . This malignity of opposition and proximity of danger, however, are like oil to the fire of my zeal." As he so often stated, he had to "obey the voice from Heaven, whether men will hear or whether they will forbear."[32]

It was his duty to press forward "the strife of Christ against the empire of Satan." In carrying out this duty opposition was inevitable. Christ and the Apostles were his models. They were persecuted for telling the truth. He was persecuted "for preaching the abominable and dangerous doctrine that all men are created equal."[33]

As the schism of 1840 made clear, Garrison often stood almost alone even among abolitionists: "Strong foes are without, insidious plotters are within the camp." The crisis evoked from him one of his own best descriptions of prophetic rhetoric. The threat from internal foes required him to "speak trumpet-tongued, sound an alarm bell, light up a beacon-fire."[34] The wheat, no matter how small the amount, had to be separated from the chaff.

The churches, he believed, were against him. Although by the 1850s the Presbyterian, Methodist, and Congregationalist churches had become major forces in the abolitionist movement, in the early years ministers and their congregations for the most part took coolly to the idea of emancipation, especially in its Garrisonian version. They sometimes actively organized themselves to oppose Garrison, as happened in Massachusetts in 1837. Undaunted by clerical criticism, Garrison and his disciples never hesitated to take on the churches, which according to them had become thoroughly corrupted through their tolerance of slavery. At its critical meeting in 1840 the American Anti-Slavery Society, inspired by Garrison, resolved that the American Church "ought not to be regarded and treated as the Church of Christ, but as a foe of freedom, humanity and pure religion, so long as it occupies its present position." Ten years later the Massachusetts Anti-Slavery Society, declaring that the American churches were not Christian bodies, called for "nothing less than a Reformation of the Religion of this Country."[35]

To take on the churches was one thing, but to take on the Constitution of the United States was another. Garrison and his followers, as well as other abolitionists, took the words of the Declaration of Independence as the authoritative source that gave utterance to their cause, justified it beyond need for justification, and sent them into battle for it: "We hold these truths to be self-evident, that all men are created equal, that they are endowed by their Creator with certain unalienable rights, that among these are life, liberty and the pursuit of happiness."

In contrast to the Declaration stood the compromise of the Constitution that seemed to allow that some men were not created equal. Garrison exploited the discrepancy and in 1854 dramatized it in a way that today would certainly land him in prison. In a speech at Framingham, Massachusetts, on July 4, he produced the Fugitive Slave Law, held a match to it, and burned it. After burning a few other documents he finally held up the Constitution, which he denounced as a betrayal of the truth, "a covenant with death, and an agreement with hell." As with the Fugitive Slave Law, he set it on fire, and while the document blazed he cried, "So perish all compromise with tyranny! And let all the people say Amen!" The large audience responded with a tremendous shout. If there were dissenting voices, they could not be heard.

Two years later, in 1856, he not only repeated in the *Liberator* his description of the Constitution as "a covenant with death and an agreement with hell" but added, anticipating a cry heard over a century later, in the 1970s, "Today, I disown the American flag as the symbol of unequaled hypocrisy and transcendent oppression."

Even if Garrison was still considered an extremist at that point, more and more people in the North were finding slavery incompatible with their consciences and with what they believed the nation stood for. More and more clergy and others were speaking out against it, and probably more effectively than Garrison. Nonetheless, Garrison was responsible for shining a glaring light on the problem for thirty years. The circulation of the *Liberator* remained small, but its name and its message were well known, partly because Southerners' so violently denounced it. There were other abolitionist newspapers, but the *Liberator* stands out among them simply by being the most uncompromising and strident.

The "immediatists," with Garrison at their head, were good propagandists for themselves and for the role they played in all that led up to the Thirteenth Amendment to the Constitution in 1865. They were in fact a relatively small minority within a movement ever more widely supported in the North and West. Even so, Garrison did help galvanize the nation, playing into its evangelical Protestantism.

For all his memorable utterances, however, Garrison was not to produce the words that best summed up the profound, messianic sense of mission that the abolition movement had generated by 1861. That was the achievement of Julia Ward Howe, the wife of a prominent Boston abolitionist who was just as committed to the cause as was Garrison but disagreed with him on many points. In the early days of the Civil War she visited a Union Army camp in Virginia where she heard soldiers singing a tribute to the abolitionist "martyr" John Brown. She was inspired to write a poem about the holy purpose of the war. In one sitting she produced her verses and sent them to the *Atlantic Monthly,* where they were published in February 1862, given the title "The Battle Hymn of the Republic," and later set to the music of a rousing camp-meeting hymn.

The words and the music quickly caught on as the anthem to rally the Union troops—and later to rally Americans behind other efforts, including the Civil Rights movement in the 1960s, when the full goal implicit in abolition moved closer to completion. In the "Hymn" cultures three and four had moved in, uninvited certainly by Garrison, to give added force to the stern prophetic message and its summons to action:

> He has sounded forth the trumpet
>   that shall never call retreat;
> He is sifting out the hearts of men
>   before His judgment-seat. . . .
> As He died to make men holy,
>   let us die to make men free,
> While God is marching on!

The abolitionists lost interest in the fate of the slaves once they were emancipated. In the South the former slaves and their descendants, though free, labored under many civil disabilities. In the North practical lines of segregation were rigorously enforced by social custom. In the country at large, blacks were supposed to "know their place"—and to stay there.

In the middle of the twentieth century the Civil Rights movement picked up where the abolitionists left off. It took aim at those parts of the South where blacks were denied access to schools, restaurants, theaters, and other public places. It took aim at segregation practices that reserved sections of buses and other means of public transportation exclusively for whites. It took aim at complicated voting systems that in effect disenfranchised blacks. It also attacked the unspoken, practical segregation operative in the North.

Martin Luther King, Jr., is the person we automatically associate with the movement. In 1954 he became pastor of a Baptist church in Montgomery, Alabama. The very next year he led a protest movement against segregation on the city buses that lasted a year, brought him national attention, and ended in victory when Montgomery desegregated its buses.

He was now positioned to be a leader in a campaign for desegregation on the broader stage of the nation and to demand equal rights not only on paper but in practice. Inspired in part by Ghandi, he advocated a policy of action through nonviolent passive resistance. In so doing he made success largely dependent on his ability to rouse folks to join in the campaign and to sustain them in it when they met resistance and even threats to their lives. As the son of a pastor and a pastor himself, bearing the name of a great prophet, King had the resources to do precisely that.

His speeches are not sermons, but behind them obviously hovered many years of experience in the pulpit and even a self-conscious appropriation of the voice of the prophets of ancient Israel. In his most famous speech, delivered on the steps of the Lincoln Memorial in Washington on August 24, 1963, he quoted without identifying it the famous passage from Isaiah: "I have a dream that one day every valley shall be exalted, every hill and mountain shall be made low, the rough places will be made plain, and the crooked places straight, and the glory of the Lord shall be revealed, and all flesh shall see it together."[36]

King held out promises of better times to come, but only if the present evil situation was overcome. He was engaged in a great "confrontation between good and evil."[37] Prophet-like, he promised a new world of justice and freedom. Like Garrison, but in an entirely different key, he rejected gradualism and insisted that the time was now for the breakthrough to freedom. In that same speech he said: "We have come [to Washington] to demand the riches of freedom and the security of justice. We have come to this hallowed spot to remind America of the fierce urgency of now. This is no time to engage in the luxury of cooling off or to take the tranquilizing drug of gradualism. Now is the time to rise from the dark and desolate valley of segregation to the sunlit path of racial justice."[38]

The next year, at the end of a massive march of thousands in Montgomery, he delivered another speech that ended with a quotation from the last stanzas of Julia Ward Howe's "Battle Hymn of the Republic." The saddest and most dramatic testimony to the power of this prophet's rhetoric and to the threat it posed is that in Memphis, Tennessee, on April 4, 1968, an end was put to it with an assassin's bullet.

Since then the prophetic impulse has continued to manifest itself in big ways and small, in noble and ignoble causes, in both secular and religious spheres. The patterns of prophetic rhetoric are also with us still. They are sometimes clearly discernible, as with TV evangelists and ranting commentators on AM radio, but they also operate somewhat less obviously in political discourse. Those patterns often deserve the skepticism and contempt they even more often evoke.

Yet when the cause is just, nothing other than the inflated rhetoric of the prophet, it seems, can shock us out of our complacency and shove before our eyes in all their starkness the alternatives we need to face. It forces us to confront them and to take a stand one way or the other, no wiggle. It also offers hope when the cause seems hopeless and when all the calculation has come to naught. It galvanizes us to action against seemingly insuperable odds because the prophets who wield this rhetoric have a dream that conveys them and us to places where we otherwise would never have the courage to go.

CULTURE TWO

The Academy and the Professions

PHILOSOPHY was already a highly developed discipline in the world into which Christianity was born. It was also a confusing discipline owing to the multiplication of schools, with Stoics, Skeptics, Pythagoreans, Platonists, and Aristotelians proffering seemingly contradictory solutions to some of the same basic issues. No matter how different those solutions were, however, all the schools were heirs to the struggle in ancient Greece, so well exemplified in the dialogues of Plato, to unmask bad arguments and to establish a basis for good ones. The process began when the Pre-Socratics questioned traditional opinions and their fellow philosophers. In Plato's dialogues what emerges most unmistakably about Socrates is his relentless questioning. If the prophetic culture is founded on the authority of "I-say-unto-you," this culture is based on probing precisely that foundation. It replies to the prophet, "Why should I accept your 'I-say-unto-you'? On what basis do you know what you say you know?" The motivation for the probing might well be to reestablish on a sounder foundation the truths in question, but the dynamic at work is centered in the process of questioning.

In the *Apology* Socrates asks to be allowed to conduct himself with one of his accusers, Meletus, "in my customary way." He goes on: "Is there anyone in the world, Meletus, who believes in human activities, and not in human beings? Make him answer, gentlemen, and don't let him keep on making these continual objections. Is there anyone who does not believe in horses, but believes in horses' activities? Or who does not believe in musicians, but believes in musical activities? . . . Is there anyone who believes in supernatural activities and not in supernatural beings?"[1] One question after the other, his "customary way." In the making is a style of discourse based on questioning.

Socrates' great merit is his probing, his making evident the flimsy basis on which "opinions" were based and statements made. Later Aristotle took the next step by analyzing the processes of reasoning and of laying out in detail what constituted sound argument. But he, Plato, and other philosophers also went about constructing designs or systems that attempted to explain the world and human conduct in a coherent and rationally defensible way. Although the philosophers differed among themselves on many points and tended to get lost within their systems, they were in the process of forming a distinctive culture in which inquiry, disagreement, and proliferation of viewpoints would be characteristic. Theirs is the culture of the inquisitive mind intolerant of sloppy thinking.

Christians and the Philosophers

Christians had to deal with this reality. They were themselves in the process of building a culture based on accepting the words and deeds of the prophet Jesus and of collecting and authorizing a group of sacred texts that would enshrine those words and deeds for posterity. They professed, moreover, to be in continuity with the prophetic culture of the Hebrew Scriptures, whose fulfillment they believed came with Jesus. It is not surprising that some Christian thinkers rejected "philosophy" as contrary to their enterprise.

They had a wisdom from on high and did not need "the wisdom of this world."

The wonder is that so many Christians were comfortable with the wisdom of this world and of its philosophers. The educated among them accepted the premises of "the philosophers" and used arguments and vocabulary similar to theirs. Justin Martyr, who converted to Christianity in the early decades of the second century, was, like Socrates, put on trial for his beliefs—his Christian beliefs. In imitation of Socrates' *Apology* he wrote two of his own, in which his words often echo the philosopher's: "Common sense dictates that they who are truly pious men and philosophers should honor and cherish only what is true and refuse to follow the beliefs of their forefathers, if these beliefs be worthless. For sound reason not only demands that we do not heed those who did or taught anything wrong, but it requires that the lover of truth must do and say what is right, even when threatened with death, rather than save his own life."[2]

"Sound reason" and "lover of truth"—these are not casual expressions. Before his conversion Justin had studied all the major philosophies, finding most satisfaction in the Platonists, and after his conversion he opened a philosophical school in Rome. His writings betray not only his knowledge of the field but, most important, his grasp and acceptance of the central tenet of culture two: the preeminence of truth and the dignity of the quest for it. As he said of Crescens the Cynic, "he proves himself to be not a lover of wisdom, but a lover of false opinions, who disregards that praiseworthy saying of Socrates: 'But no man must be honored before the truth.'"[3]

Justin had of course studied philosophy not as a Christian but as a pagan. But born Christians had no qualms in doing so. If such study was incompatible with their faith, they with few exceptions gave no evidence they were aware of it. They had been born into "Athens." The first and fundamental education that boys received in the Hellenistic world was literary or "humanistic." Nonetheless, in late antiquity, particularly in the East, small numbers of ambitious youths moved on to a formal study of philosophy for a year or more at the end of their rhetorical education, usually when they were in their late teens. They did so in schools designed for that purpose, which is to say they did so under a teacher who for a fee offered lectures in a given philosophical tradition or was even paid from public funds to do so. (There were similar schools for law, medicine, and architecture.) Sophisticated though the instruction might be in given instances, these were basically one-room schoolhouses, though at certain times and places, especially in Athens and Alexandria, a school might be more elaborate. A stunning exception was the imperial school at Constantinople founded in 425 that lasted, with periods of decline and temporary extinction, until 1453. At its inception it consisted of twenty grammarians, eight rhetoricians, two lawyers, but, for all its grandiosity, only one philosopher.

Just as it never seemed to occur to Christians from the upper classes not to study the "pagan" literature that was the backbone of the curriculum, it never occurred to them not to study the great philosophers if they wanted to put the finishing touches on their education. It was what one did. Seemingly without misgiving they enrolled under teachers and sat side-by-side with students who often were not Christian.

For the most part, then, educated Christians looked upon philosophy as religiously neutral. Although at Athens it sometimes took on an anti-Christian bias, at Alexandria there was an especially strong tradition of avoiding both polemic and apologetic. It was this neutrality that accounts for the survival of Alexandrian Aristotelianism after the Arab conquest, and its subsequent survival in Baghdad, with great consequences for its revival in the West in the twelfth century.

Even when Christians themselves taught philosophy during the patristic era, they seem to have stuck to the traditional task of simply explaining a text without trying to give it a Christian spin. After Origen, a born Christian, left Alexandria in 231, he taught philosophy for a while at Caesarea, where Gregory Thaumaturgus, the future bishop and saint, was one of his pupils. Through Origen Gregory converted to Christianity, but Origen in his lectures seems to have given philosophers their say and encouraged his students' curiosity. Here is how Gregory recounted the experience: "For us there was nothing forbidden, nothing hidden, nothing inaccessible. We were allowed to learn every doctrine, Greek and non-Greek, both spiritual and secular, both divine and human. With the utmost freedom we went into everything and examined it thoroughly, taking our fill of and enjoying the pleasures of the soul."[4]

Philosophy in itself might be neutral, but Christians began to discover that studying it sometimes led students on to the more perfect "philosophy" taught by Christ. In antiquity teachers of philosophy generally tried to create an atmosphere in the classrooms that seems almost religious, filled with reverence for the texts and conducive to reflection and a life lived in conformity with the teaching of the texts. In its avowed practitioners philosophy meant first of all a way of life, a way dedicated to the truths upon which they discoursed. In the Acts of the Apostles the first Christians described themselves as following "a way," which, when compared later with the philosophical "ways" of Athens, they saw as far superior but not necessarily or always antithetical. It was an easy but astounding step to begin to describe Christianity itself as a philosophy.

This existential aspect of philosophy would remain strong in Christianity until the founding of the universities. But in this early period, besides the questioning that philosophy entailed, the content and more elaborated methods of philosophy soon came to immediate uses for the Christian community. Even by the third century the community was wracked with doctrinal disputes, whose solutions seemed to require the systematic and technical approach that philosophy promised. Thus almost from the beginning there was a current that in one way or another tried to harness philosophical concepts for Christian needs. At its headwaters stands Origen, a younger contemporary of Tertullian. Although the beginnings of a systematic approach can be detected in writers before him, the very title of his work *On First Principles (De principiis)* suggests a philosophical perspective.

Even with what we know about the infiltration of Aristotelian ideas into the circles in which Origen moved, his early career as a *grammaticus,* a teacher of poetry, would seem to make him an unlikely candidate for writing the *First Principles.* His first foundation, therefore, was solidly in culture three, and his writings, especially his homilies, show it unmistakably. But in him, as in most thinkers of the era, the boundaries between cultures two and three were permeable.

In *First Principles* the language is in fact nontechnical and accessible, and only if one is already familiar with the Aristotelian ideal of "science" can one detect how it structures what Origen is about. His Platonism is more easily detectable. Nonetheless, especially in this book he reveals knowledge of Aristotle's corpus, including the works on natural philosophy. Most important, the book implicitly aims at establishing a method for resolving controversies about the contents of the Christian faith as contained in the Scriptures. The method is based on two essential elements in the Aristotelian ideal for a science, that is, a rationally convincing body of knowledge: first, it must be derived from "first principles" agreed upon as true; second, by logical argumentation the relationship of these principles with one another must be shown to result in a coherent whole. That is precisely the project Origen sketches in his preface: "Everyone therefore who is desirous of constructing out of the foregoing a connected body of doctrine must use points like these as elementary and foundation principles. . . . Thus, by clear and cogent arguments he will discover the truth about each particular point and so will produce, as we have said, a single body of doctrine, with the aid of such illustrations and declarations as he shall find in the Scriptures and of such conclusions as he shall ascertain to follow logically from them when rightly understood."[5]

He will proceed by "clear and cogent arguments." He will construct "a connected body of doctrine." In so doing he will make use of "conclusions" that follow "logically." The *First Principles* is, then, constructed on a *method.* The method is a Christian adaptation of Aristotle. Though prompted by controversies over what constituted essential Christian teaching, it is not, as such, a polemical work. It is, rather, "academic." Origen has a theory about the Christian faith, and his book is an illustration of how the theory works. His theory is that the corpus of basic Christian beliefs is internally coherent and consistent. Its basic presuppositions, therefore, are that such a coherence inheres in those beliefs and that the coherence is discoverable by the human mind. Origen sets out in a systematic, dispassionate way to demonstrate the workings of those presuppositions. No loose ends, no unsubstantiated assertions, no resort to paradox. The *First Principles,* though obviously stemming from deeply felt religious sentiment and generally couched in nontechnical language, is an appeal to the mind.

The *First Principles,* a work of utmost importance for the future of Christian theology, was well known in the West through a somewhat tendentious Latin translation done by Rufinus a century and a half later, the only complete text now surviving. Even when the kind of intellectual ideal it modeled almost receded from memory in the Latin West, the *First Principles* stood as a reminder of a certain way of addressing issues. It provided a model for orderly approach to theological problems that would be used by writers who had no familiarity with Aristotle.

For more than two centuries after Origen, Aristotle himself remained at best a subtext in Christian writers in the East and especially in the West. But toward the end of the fifth century a remarkable change began to take place in Alexandria, where for a considerable period Aristotle took on a commanding role in the approach of Greek-speaking theologians. At the radiating center of Alexandria a publicly paid teacher of philosophy named Ammonius held forth for more than forty years beginning in 480. Ammonius, not a Christian himself, had many Christian disciples.

For those disciples the time was ripe for the highly technical definition of terms required by Aristotle for valid argument. Doctrinal controversies among Christians had intensified, not died down, since the days of Origen. Only by means of the precise language that philosophy provided could orthodoxy be clearly distinguished from heterodoxy, as was clear in 325 in the documents of the first great Christian council at Nicea.

Although Ammonius' basic scheme of the universe was Neo-Platonic, the distinctive feature of his teaching and of the whole Alexandrian school for the next century was the philosophy of Aristotle. Christians moving in that milieu came to believe that Aristotle supplied the equipment now needed to deal with further questions and controversies. They were ready to do the work to appropriate his teaching.

Their diligence effected a transformation in the Christian intellectual enterprise in the East that lasted for several centuries. Theology, up to that time for the most part an outgrowth of preaching (as it would essentially remain in the West until the late twelfth century), now developed into a self-consciously intellectual discipline. Writers were proud to argue "in an Aristotelian manner." Precise definition of terms assumed a dominating importance—no ambiguity. The syllogism became the preferred tool for correct argumentation, used without apology. Examples used to illustrate points at issue were no longer borrowed from everyday life, as in the more homiletic style of theological argument, but from Aristotle's technical works on physics, psychology, and astronomy.

Knowledge of the physical world, as analyzed and codified by Aristotle, was thus requisite.

For Christianity a new intellectual style had emerged, as manifested in a new style of discourse—argumentative, lean, technical, heady. Terms were subjected to the most rigorous analysis, and systematic arguments were developed from non-Scriptural sources. In all this the writers foreshadowed in a remarkable way medieval Scholastic theology. To read a paragraph from them is to realize that one has entered an intellectual world fundamentally different even from that of the *First Principles.*

This style did not catch on in the West, partly because of seemingly endemic antipathy to the highly technical style of Aristotle and partly because of the gravely unsettled political and cultural situation brought on by the collapse of Roman imperial institutions, which in turn meant even further decline in the ability to read Greek. Nonetheless, at Ravenna a conduit of surpassing importance appeared that would save the ideal from falling into utter oblivion—Boethius.

Born in Rome probably in 480, the year Ammonius began teaching, Boethius as a young adult possibly studied in Alexandria for a brief period. He feared that amid the general collapse of learning of his times the great knowledge acquired by the philosophers and scientists of Athens would be lost simply by a failure of transmission. To do his part to remedy the situation, he planned to translate into Latin the entire corpus of Plato and Aristotle, but his early death at the age of forty-four meant he succeeded only with a few of Aristotle's treatises on logic.

As the completed portion of his project shows, he was fascinated by "reason," that is, by the process and rules of correct thinking leading to proof for one's argument. He managed to compose at least four original theological works, all of which exhibit traits consonant with this fascination and with the style of theological reasoning developing at Alexandria. These works are not the incontestable assertions of the prophet. They are not the ruminations or exhortations of culture three. They are not ritual performances. They are works of theory and abstract speculation.

"Since no relation can be related to itself, inasmuch as one that makes a predication by itself is a predication that lacks relation," says Boethius in his book on the Trinity, "the manifoldness of the Trinity is produced in the fact that it is predication of a relation, and the unity is preserved through the fact that there is no difference of substance, or operation, or generally of that kind of predication that is made on its own."[6] That sentence reveals without need of comment the abstract, technical, and learned world and its style of discourse that Boethius almost single-handedly in the West salvaged, appropriated, and transmitted. It represents culture two in its most severe and uncompromising mode.

Here is a cultural ideal that has adopted categories and methods from Athens and assumed without significant hesitation that they were on some level compatible with Jerusalem, even necessary for its well-being. Boethius did not, of course, think that Christian beliefs like the Trinity and Incarnation could be found in the philosophers, but he did believe that the philosophers could help toward some understanding of such truths and especially protect them from the corruption of heresy. Insofar as Christian truths were dogmatic, that is, accepted on faith in prophetic authority, what Boethius is effecting is a takeover or at least a taming of culture one by culture two. This is what Luther saw clearly in Scholastic theologians, Boethius' medieval counterparts, and he cried in outrage against it.

Boethius' influence was incalculable. In the early Middle Ages Christians, in small numbers, pored over his texts, especially the translations, but his influence reached a peak in the twelfth century right at the moment when new Latin translations of Aristotle's other works were arriving in Paris and elsewhere. It was "the age of Boethius." His works became central "in the schools." He stimulated that thoroughgoing study of the reasoning process so prominent in the age, and he taught medieval thinkers the importance of precision, order, and care in the use of words. He provided a model for the style of discourse that came to prevail in Scholasticism. Thomas Aquinas paid him the honor of writing commentaries on his *De trinitate* and *De hebdomatibus* and openly acknowledged his debt to him. A passage from his commentary on the latter work illustrates the orderly and reasoned model that caught on: "[Boethius] therefore states first that he intends to propose from the start certain kinds of principles, known through themselves, which he calls *terms* and *rules:* 'terms' because the resolution back to prior principles of all demonstrations stops at principles of this sort; 'rules,' however, because through them one is directed to a knowledge of conclusions which follow. From principles of this sort he intends to draw conclusions and to make known all that ought to be developed as following logically, as happens in geometry and in other demonstrative sciences."[7]

Above all, Boethius made scholars' minds hungry for even more Aristotle and prepared them to appreciate him when he was finally within their grasp. Without the softening up for Aristotle that Boethius provided, it is difficult to imagine that "the philosopher" would so quickly have risen to intellectual preeminence. And without Aristotle it is difficult to imagine what that momentous turning point in the cultural history of the West, the founding of the universities, would otherwise have looked like, had it occurred at all.

The Birth of Academic Culture

The development of Western academic life, for all its debt to classical antiquity, is the more direct heir of phenomena that began to take discernible shape in the twelfth century and reached a significant articulation in the thirteenth. The tenth century and then more firmly the eleventh sent out signals that things were changing for the better after all the West had suffered from the disintegration of Roman institutions and seemingly endless incursions from north, south, and east. The recovery included and was presaged by the keener and more systematic interest in law that preceded, accompanied, and followed the Gregorian Reform.

The change included a more patent appreciation for classical authors. At Rheims Gerbert of Aurillac (d. 1003), later Pope Sylvester II, read Virgil, Statius, Terence, Juvenal, Persius, Horace, and Lucan with his students. While at Rheims he also seems to have been the first master since antiquity to use logical works of Aristotle and Boethius as integral to his curriculum. By 1079 St. Anselm had written both the *Monologion* and the *Proslogion,* followed by that remarkable series of philosophical and theological works culminating in 1098 with *Cur Deus homo,* "Why God Became Man," a title that is an implicit question. By 1028 Fulbert had created a cathedral school at Chartres that for a century and a half could boast of an unbroken tradition of brilliant teachers and writers, but other cathedral schools were also coming into their own. They were the seedbeds from which the universities would spring. Young men were on the move from city to city to listen to teachers whose reputations had somehow or other traveled hundreds and hundreds of miles to reach them, often in remote places.

It is in the twelfth century, however, that all this ferment began to take recognizable shape. Among other things, it soon led to the creation of the university and with it, the permanent and prominent securing in Western civilization of a highly professionalized and certified style of learning. In that century young men manifested in astounding numbers three psychological traits that must be taken into account if we are to understand what happened.

First, for whatever reason, these young men were mad for learning, searching for it wherever it might be found, searching for it especially in teachers who could help them assimilate it. They were almost undiscriminating in that their curiosity ranged over almost every conceivable object of knowledge, but they showed an especially keen interest in the physical world, a world newly revealed to them as Aristotle's works on subjects like physics and astronomy became available. By 1200 the West had the entire Aristotelian corpus in Latin except the *Ethics, Politics,* and parts of the *Metaphysics.* A century earlier a certain Constantinus Africanus had translated a number of Greek and Arabic medical works, which became standard textbooks. In Italy compilations of Roman law were long known, but only at the beginning of the twelfth century did Irnerius begin at Bologna to lecture on Roman civil law, the *Corpus iuris civilis,* and to produce detailed and well-regarded commentaries on it. These rediscovered texts jolted the minds of twelfth-century scholars like an electric charge.

The second remarkable trait of these generations was their passion for order, so clearly manifested in their pursuit of legal texts, ecclesiastical and civil. The Gregorians studied such texts, after all, because they wanted to restore the "right" order to society. The ultimate goal was to establish just and proper procedures for the management of the affairs of society, civil and religious, but this meant putting order into the often chaotic collections of the very documents that promised to provide orderly procedures. Sometimes the documents seemed to contradict one another. The great landmark in making sense of ecclesiastical legislation that in the process also provided a paradigm for dealing with the corpus of civil law was Gratian's *Decretum,* completed about 1140. It both summarized the legal wisdom of the ecclesiastical establishment up to that point and tried to bring "concordance to the discordant canons" that expressed that wisdom. In the *Decretum* Gratian took a big step in transforming the study of canon law from an ill-defined branch of sacred learning into an independent legal science. The *Decretum* was, however, only one of a handful of texts that by acting in effect as minilibraries allowed scholars to move beyond the past to be positioned to see further.

Among such texts was Peter Lombard's *Sentences,* a book that organized into headings Christian teaching as it had hitherto been discussed by the Fathers of the Church with, again, an attempt to resolve discrepancies. It was an unprecedented innovation, though some writers like Origen had pointed the way. Topically arranged in a logical system, the first-ever such arrangement for Christian doctrines, the *Sentences* in their very structure exemplify the momentous cultural shift that was under way. As would be true with the other great texts of the period, especially the *summae,* the medium was indeed as significant as the content.

Its style of discourse fits the pattern of abstract reasoning. Here's a typical passage, dealing with the Trinity: "The rational mind, when it must consider something triple yet one, is contemplating the Creator where it sees unity in trinity and trinity in unity. It understands that God is one—one essence, one principle. It understands that if there were two Gods, one would be deficient or the other superfluous. If something were lacking in one that the other had, that one would not have the supreme perfection that is God; but if nothing were lacking that the other had, which means it had everything, the other would be superfluous."[8]

The third of these traits, clearly manifested in the early twelfth century but obvious long before and even more impressive later, was the impulse to join together in voluntary groups to achieve a common purpose. Medieval men and women were inveterate joiners. The stereotype of that society as essentially top-down is far from the mark. Popes, kings and queens, bishops, duchesses and dukes, with their retainers, their elaborate entourages, and their battles sometimes crowd out everything else in our historical imagination, as we forget how contained by custom and other constraints the authority of these figures was and how little structural change most of these offices effected in how society operated. Though these vertical threads were without argument of crucial importance, the horizontal threads were what in many ways wove the fabric of medieval society together. Society functioned through a network of voluntary associations among peers.

The list of such groups is long. Monasteries are among the most obvious. When the monasteries had passed their apogee, men and women joined the mendicant orders like the Franciscans and the Dominicans, orders remarkable for their "democratic" form of governance. As cities revived, the inhabitants joined together in parishes, which came into being not by episcopal mandate but by the desire of neighbors to join together in worship. They joined together in confraternities for their spiritual betterment and mutual assistance. Merchants, traders, and artisans joined in guilds.

These voluntary associations in an age ever more concerned with legal procedures sought appropriate legal status from the appropriate authorities. They provided for their own protection by seeking from popes, kings, bishops, and municipalities a guarantee for the "liberties and immunities" they needed to operate. They were otherwise independent and self-regulating, and for the most part they turned out to be the most highly successful "clubs" the world has ever seen.

Among them, of course, is the university, which by the end of the twelfth century had achieved a remarkably mature organization at Bologna and at Paris, the former a guild of students, the latter principally of masters. These two were soon emulated and then adapted in other cities. By the end of the Middle Ages eighty institutions that can be considered universities had proudly established themselves across Western and Central Europe. Along with church and state, the university was sometimes reckoned as the third power in medieval society—*regnum, sacerdotium, studium.* Rectors of universities had scepters, visible signs of their autonomous and considerable authority.

In the second half of the twelfth century two realities thus developed simultaneously and symbiotically—an institution and a style of learning. The style of learning found its natural home in the institution. The style of the learning was systematic; the institution was organized in a systematic way precisely in order systematically to foster such learning. Both these realities built upon foundations from late antiquity that had survived or somehow been recovered, and they both more immediately grew out of developments earlier in the century. They were, nonetheless, quantum leaps beyond what preceded them.

The university created, to a degree and in a way never known before, the publicly certified professional, whether in law, medicine, theology, or "Arts." It created a new social class, small in numbers but not in prestige. Although it had its more practical aspects in law and medicine, it brought them to an incomparably sharper and more differentiated articulation. It fostered the culture of the intellectual, culture two, and provided it with a quite special venue, a corporation. It thereby delivered it to an engine of propagation propelled by an intrinsically dynamic method of inquiry.

By the early decades of the thirteenth century, the university had established its prestige. It was *the* school. More informal styles of learning of course persisted, as was especially true for medicine. The apprenticeship system continued in this field as in others, including the sciences, almost into the twentieth century. No later than the early thirteenth century, however, university-trained physicians and lawyers, especially those who had completed the full course and held a degree, enjoyed a prestige and could command fees denied to others. Students went to the universities to learn, but with rare exception the desire to learn was propelled by a desire to make a career. With a degree they carried with them proof of their competence and of having negotiated their way through a demanding and complex program of study.

What is astounding about the university is not only the complex and highly sophisticated degree of organization it manifested and the clarity of the goals each of its component parts set for itself but also the rapidity with which these achievements were attained, even if we grant great influence from Islamic models. In a very short time the university came into being with a full array of officers, a full complement of teachers, elaborate programs of study, texts to accompany the programs, and all the rules and regulations required to keep the programs on course. An institution had been established whose basic structure and ethos would persist for centuries and remarkably reassert itself in our own day.

Although a degree in Arts was not always an absolute prerequisite for a degree in the other faculties, candidates in those faculties needed to have a grounding in the subjects taught in it. A degree in Arts, esteemed in its own right, also served as a kind of preprofessional degree. Students generally entered the Arts faculty in their early or mid-teens, with the only prerequisite an ability to read Latin. If they stayed to complete the bachelor's degree, they needed something like four years or more, at least two more for the master's. A bachelor's degree in medicine might take three to six years more. At Paris theology was by far the most exacting. After the Arts degree or its equivalent, the student of theology needed some fifteen or more years to work his way through the bachelor's degree to the doctorate. But these times differed widely from university to university, especially in the later Middle Ages, and "quicky" degrees were not unknown.

Arts, in any case, was the faculty in which all students had to spend time. As the name indicates, the seven "liberal arts" of the trivium (grammar, rhetoric, logic) and quadrivium (arithmetic, geometry, astronomy, music) supposedly constituted the core of the curriculum. But at Paris, for instance, philosophy—or "the three philosophies"—early on began to dominate everything else. The three philosophies or aspects of philosophy were natural (the physical sciences), moral (ethics), and metaphysical. At Paris arithmetic, basic to the quadrivium, was taught mainly on feast days, not regular class days, and music was taught in an unmitigatedly theoretical way, with no performance.

Aristotle's logical works, which included dialectics, were of course known and studied long before his works on natural philosophy, ethics, or metaphysics, so it is not surprising that logic, one of the elements in the trivium, was considered the gateway into those "three philosophies." As a subject required of every student in the Arts faculty, logic thus turned out to be the grounding for discourse not only in that faculty but in the other three as well. At Paris it began to overrun and condition the other two elements in the trivium. True, grammar and to some extent rhetoric continued to be taught, but with logic heavily influencing how they were interpreted and applied.

A practical repercussion of this development was that "grammar," which the ancients and earlier medievals understood as the study of language and literature, got so transformed that literature as such was virtually excluded from the curriculum. Poetry, the traditional subject under the heading of grammar, was therefore little taught, and drama, history, and oratory not at all. At Paris and the universities following the Parisian model, rhetoric fared only slightly better. At Bologna and universities following its model, these disciplines were more cultivated, which explains why these universities would later in the Renaissance be more amenable to the humanists' demands for a place for literature in the curriculum. Generally speaking, however, the universities developed in ways that made holders of the Master of Arts degree, despite that title, tone-deaf to culture three. In their teaching those masters were even further removed from art and performance, culture four.

Master of Arts degree! What an underestimated innovation degrees were. If a culture is in part a configuration of symbols, then the centering symbol of this culture was the degree, the public recognition of mastery. Yet the degree was only one of many other symbols that in the thirteenth century seemed to rush into place in universities across Europe—distinctive gowns, distinctive hats, rings for the finger, scepters for rectors, seals, statute books, special holidays and feasts, ceremonies of induction, highly ritualized rites of passage known as examinations. Above all, perhaps, there were the daily or almost daily rituals of lecture and disputation, of glossing texts and commenting upon them, then of moving along for years in a prescribed path filled with written and unwritten rules of the game that resulted in ways of thinking and talking, in ways of appreciating reality, that were distinctive and that often rendered the discourse unintelligible to outsiders.

What, in somewhat more detail, were some features of those distinctive ways? In all the faculties of the university the study was based on texts, principally Greek and Arabic translated into Latin. This was true even for the faculty of medicine, where apprenticeship to a senior physician and attendance at anatomical demonstrations on the human cadaver were also an essential part of the training. In all the faculties the texts were approached in a highly systematic way, with well-defined tools of analysis and argument ratified by the consensus of the corporation.

The text-base of the enterprise fostered a theoretical and speculative style of learning. Although the university was ultimately meant to relate to practical life and even contribute to the good of society by training professionals, unlike the later humanistic schools it never articulated its philosophy of education for this or any other aspect of its reality. The faculties of law and medicine had the obviously practical sides to them, though especially law had some not so obvious practical functions, such as providing training for notaries that made for efficient clerks and estate managers, men who knew how to keep books and draw up contracts.

Theology was supposed to serve, among other things, as a training for preachers. It was these academics, after all, who produced the first real handbooks dealing with every aspect of the preaching enterprise, the *Artes praedicandi,* which were unmitigatedly practical, how-to books. As the faculties of theology evolved over time, they performed another social service, monitoring the orthodoxy of their colleagues. They came to be the recognized body for this task, performing it on a more regular basis than did the episcopacy or the papacy. (It is perhaps helpful to recall, however, that in the "Christian Middle Ages" practically all universities had faculties of law, whereas relatively few had faculties of theology.)

But a truly central feature in the university enterprise was the pursuit of "ideas" and the recognition that this pursuit was at least a step removed from immediate application. Theology, Aquinas assured his readers in the opening question of his *Summa theologiae,* is in the first instance a "speculative" discipline. The *Summa* is a work of theology without obvious connection to the practice of Christian ministry.

The *summa* is a genre of which Aquinas' is only one example. The genre exemplifies—in its very structure and assumptions even more so than in its content—the salient characteristics of culture two. At the core of that culture is the imperative to listen to opposing viewpoints and to engage in dialectical commerce with them. What has Athens to do with Jerusalem? The texts of Aristotle and his great Arab commentators excited curiosity but also fear. They contradicted the Bible on several key issues, such as the doctrine of the creation of the world. Beginning in 1210 with the Council of Sens, bishops and prelates issued for Paris a series of prohibitions of Aristotle's works on natural philosophy. Other condemnations and prohibitions occurred later. The great issue facing theologians was what to do with Aristotle, that is, with "reason."

"Reason" or "philosophy" here meant two things: first, the processes of reasoning and discoursing set forth in Aristotle's books on logic, and second, the information about the physical and metaphysical worlds and about politics and ethics contained in his other works as well as similar works by other ancient thinkers. "Reason" meant, therefore, both form and content. St Bernard feared the former—"dialectics"—as much as others, like the bishops at Sens, feared the latter.

While theologians in the universities would over the next few centuries differently assess just how and to what degree reconciliation was possible between "reason" and the Bible, they almost by definition could not disallow it altogether. The very language and forms of reasoning they employed to address the issue already tipped the scales toward an affirmative answer, whether they acknowledged it or not. Aquinas enjoys the deserved reputation for being not only among the most confident and bold in working out the relationship but also among the most successful.

Christians had the Bible. Why did they need Aristotle? That might seem to be the state of the question in the twelfth and thirteenth centuries. Yet Aquinas opens his *Summa* by turning the question around. We have Aristotle. Why do we need the Bible? By so turning the question Aquinas betrays how the rediscovery of Aristotle had shifted the ground of argument, not to mention how almost unquestioning was the confidence in the truth of Aristotle's grasp of reality. Despite the turn, he goes on to subscribe to an already traditional answer: the truths of Christianity go beyond what philosophy can offer and sometimes must even correct it. Athens and Jerusalem are partners, though in case of conflict the latter must prevail. Many earlier Christian thinkers had in one way or another expressed this opinion, but the new Scholastic genres like the *summae* and the *quaestiones disputatae* provided new media in which to work out in great, systematic detail either that option or a more skeptical one. The genres themselves, with their new and distinctive characteristics, were in and of themselves manifestations of the profundity of the intellectual revolution that had taken place.

The first characteristic of these genres and the majority of other works published by medieval theologians is that they were generated not out of pastoral activity, such as sermons or efforts to reply to heresies immediately pressing upon the faithful, which was true for most of the writing about sacred subjects of earlier eras. These new genres are directed to speculative concerns, detached to a large extent from the world outside the lecture halls. True, Aquinas began writing his *Summa* to help train young Dominicans for the hearing of confessions, but it soon exceeded that pastoral scope to become a work of abstract analysis and synthesis.

The *Summa* manifests other characteristics of the great shift. The title, new to this era, reveals much. As a *summa,* the book aims at comprehensiveness. It will tell you "all you need to know." It will neither omit anything nor dodge anything that is pertinent. To that extent it is a replay of what Origen attempted in the *First Principles,* but the scope has been incomparably enlarged. Every question that can be raised is pursued down to the last detail so as to satisfy every objection that can be made. Divided into "articles," it is, again, incomparably more articulated than Origen's work or any other work from the early Christian era.

Comprehensive, yes, but also coherent. All the parts fit. In his well-known essay Erwin Panofsky compared gothic architecture to works of Scholastic theology. In a gothic cathedral, despite its complexity and vastness, each rib and each buttress, each pilaster and pillar contributes to the harmony of the whole. The cathedral is coherent, just as a *summa* is coherent. No part out of place, no superfluous parts, no digressions. The coherence of Thomas' *Summa* is, in fact, stunning, intellectually beautiful—a cathedral in the mind.

How is the coherence obtained? By a complicated process, of course, but surely basic to it was the dialectical ideal of point-counterpoint, Abelard's "yes and no" *(sic et non),* searching for resolution. As Aquinas says, theology as a science is "argumentative"—it "argues" and it "proves." It in fact "disputes." Debate is the model that lurks in the background with this style of discoursing. Theology therefore argues in a dialectical way, with thesis (yes) antithesis (no), and synthesis or resolution. Such a resolution differs altogether from the mode of the prophet, who will let extremes persist side-by-side in paradoxes that defy resolution. The lion lies down with the lamb, with neither being transformed into the other or into a third thing. But in culture two, such transformations are the ideal. For Luther both bread and body are contained in the Eucharist and commingled, yet they remain distinct. For the Scholastic theologians the bread is transformed into the body, becoming a new substance—transubstantiated.

The coherence is made as patent as humanly possible, just as in a gothic cathedral all the ribs are exposed to view. Thomas immediately signals this aspect of his work by devoting the whole first Question to a discussion of method. These, he says, are my assumptions, this is what I am doing and how I am doing it. He exposes it all to view—and to possible challenge. The first thing he does in these opening lines of the book is make patent the "ten questions" about the nature of theology that he will answer in the discrete units that make up the first Question:

> 1. Whether sacred doctrine is necessary. 2. Whether it is a science. 3. Whether it is one science, or several. 4. Whether it is speculative or practical. 5. How it is related to other sciences. 6. Whether it is wisdom. 7. What is its subject matter. 8. Whether it is argumentative. 9. Whether it ought to use metaphors and figures of speech. 10. Whether the sacred Scriptures of this doctrine should be expounded in several ways.

Similar procedures typify the rest of this really big book: divided into three major Parts, each Part subdivided into hundreds of

Questions, each Question divided into five to ten or more Articles, each Article formatted into four units—possible problems with the resolution about to be offered, statement of the resolution, arguments for the resolution, and responses to each of the problems originally raised.

The medium is the message—lucidity, rationality, coherence, completeness, and order are what the whole undertaking strives for. The result is a system, an Aristotelian "science," an intellectually satisfying whole. Intellectual satisfaction is the goal Saint Anselm had set the enterprise a century earlier—"faith seeking *understanding*." That is the goal Aquinas pursues.

The intellect is not, however, easily satisfied. In northern France in the twelfth century the "question" had emerged as a tool of method, a tool peculiar to culture two from the days of Socrates but now newly formalized. It dominates the *Summa* as well as most works of Scholastic philosophy and theology. The Scholastics no longer just ruminated over their texts line-by-line, trying to understand what they said. In a systematic way they moved to a further stage. Although the interpretation of texts remained basic to what they were about and they continued to write interpretations and commentaries on texts, they now had questions that did not arise from the texts. "What does the text tell us?" got transformed into "How can we make the text answer our questions?" This had the effect of transforming the texts, including the Bible, into databases to be explored and exploited, quarries from which to cut stones to be used in the building of the intellectual cathedral.

The emergence of the "question" was obviously of momentous methodological significance. When a question got answered, the next question had to be asked. Two instruments, imperfectly distinct from each other, imbued the university enterprise with its restless dynamism. The first was the question itself, which is just a more abstract way of saying the quest—the quest for answer. The second was the syllogistic process, largely conceived, which found its most obvious manifestation in the frequent public disputations in which the masters were obliged to participate. They were by that exercise obliged to present their views to their colleagues in an open forum. It would be difficult to imagine a style of discourse more intellectually aggressive and agonistic. Dialectics, the art of winning an argument, undergirded it. The disputation gave form and anchor to two fundamental traits of academic culture from the thirteenth century forward: first, the single-minded pursuit of truth, lead where it may, and, second, almost as a corollary, the capacity to be unsparingly self-critical and hence, self-correcting.

This internal dynamism means that a work like the *Summa* is going someplace. It churns along, disposing of difficulties, delving into particulars wherever the quest leads but guided by its own overall structure of the three parts. It and other works like it are, as said, big books. They are big because of the energy inherent in their method. The *Summa* has no patience for the prophet's repetition of the same battle cry. It has no time for the poet's circling around and around the same sentiment, or the politician's recourse to "the values we all share." The *Summa* expresses the intellectual's relentless quest.

The *Summa,* by tackling all problems and disposing of all difficulties, implicitly presents itself as definitive, as if the quest were over. It has proved, "demonstrated," its conclusions. But the very nature of culture two, as so well exemplified in theologians like Aquinas, means that the *summae* themselves had to be subjected to questioning, which is precisely what happened. The dialectical process did not rest.

The theologians tried their best to stay within the confines of received beliefs, but the dynamism of their very method propelled them further. They *had* to ask the next question, and they *had* to pursue the argument to its logical conclusion. They were not, like their modern counterparts in academia, thrashing around in search of "fresh ideas." Yet their *method,* their style of discoursing, drove them to the medieval equivalent. After the middle of the twelfth century most of the noted heretics or near-heretics were products of the universities—Abelard, Arnold of Brescia, William of Ockham, Marsilius of Padua, Peter John Olivi, Eckhart, Wycliffe, Hus, and Luther himself. The canonization of Thomas Aquinas in 1322 showed that it was possible to be a university person and also be holy and orthodox, just as would the much later canonization of Bonaventure, but there was another side to the ledger.

With the emergence of the university, moreover, even theology moved to a significantly different, more secular physical space, with subtle repercussions for the future of culture two. This was the move from pulpit and cloister to classroom. Augustine, Ambrose, and Gregory the Great taught in the midst of their pastoral whirlwind. They taught in their cathedrals, vested for liturgy. Bernard and his fellow Cistercian abbots did the same in their monastery chapels. Classrooms existed in these situations, but within the cathedral close or within the monastery walls. Even as theological faculties in the universities had to rent classroom space and as residence halls arose, chapels were often in the same building or on the same grounds, as is so clear even today in universities like Oxford and Cambridge. But in principle another fatal shift had occurred. The harsh glare of fluorescent light will displace the warm glow of the candle and the soft colors streaming through the stained-glass windows: "Europe's long march toward the Age of Reason was first institutionalized in medieval universities."[9]

The ideal in the classroom, as in the *Summa,* was a detached objectivity. Philosophy in this context lost its earlier meaning as a way of life and became a collection of intellectual disciplines in which the masters disappeared behind the subject. This meant that, with few exceptions, the story of their lives as we have them is meager. Even when information is a little more ample, it consists in where they taught, with whom they debated, what books they wrote, and what positions they took on different issues. These authors have left no record of their laughter or their tears. They reasoned about the harmony of the universe. But if they felt wonder for it, the style of discourse of their profession inhibited them from expressing it.

Aquinas, Scotus, Ockham, Gregory of Rimini, Henry of Harclay—these and others left behind many writings, but they left no personal diaries. Except for a stray letter here and there, they left no correspondence. If such documents existed, neither they nor their disciples thought them worth preserving or even mentioning. These are the missing genres. They are, supposedly, inappropriate and inconsequential for culture two.

The Council of Trent

Despite indications to the contrary, in the sixteenth century the university remained the robust institution that had evolved over the previous three centuries and retained its immense prestige. Two developments, however, challenged especially the faculties of Arts and theology. The first was the resurgence of literary studies that originated in Italy with Petrarch in the mid-fourteenth century. As mentioned, the Italian university tradition showed itself relatively amenable to the refashioning of the trivium that the humanists demanded. By the second quarter of the fifteenth century humanists began holding regular teaching positions in the Arts faculties there.

By the sixteenth century the humanist movement had spread outside Italy to areas where the academic climate was much less favorable to it. This "new learning," as it was known in those places, threatened established academic traditions. The humanists insisted, among other things, on a more historical and literary approach to ancient texts, which was resisted in the faculties of law as well as in Arts and theology. Especially in the Arts faculty the humanists' criticism of how grammar and rhetoric had become the slaves of logic and dialectic threatened to unsettle time-proven procedures and to imply the need for change in both curriculum and style of pedagogy—never welcome news. It did not help matters that humanists called the academic style of discourse barbarous. Resentments flared, territory wars erupted, harsh words were exchanged. Who did these "mere grammarians" think they were?

Erasmus assumed leadership of the humanist movement early in the century, directing his criticism especially against theology. He joined in the standard criticisms of the establishment that to a greater or lesser extent had been in circulation for a long time, even outside humanist circles: the theologians were lost in their own world; they spoke an impenetrable jargon; they were constantly at one another's throats over issues of concern to nobody but themselves; they lived in their heads; they could not touch anybody's heart.

Vituperation flew in both directions, but in these sometimes no-holds-barred exchanges the humanists enjoyed the advantage of more effective appropriation of rhetorical skills. Not surprisingly Erasmus, though he often tried to pass himself off as innocent of invective, was one of the worst (that is, best) offenders. His assessment of theologians in a letter to Thomas Grey in 1497 is too delicious not to repeat: "[their] brains are the most addled, tongues the most uncultivated, wits the dullest, teachings the thorniest, characters the least attractive, lives the most hypocritical, and hearts the blackest on earth."[10]

In 1497 these maliciously clever words may not have been much more than a litterateur making fun of metaphysicians. As Erasmus matured, however, he grew to believe an unbridgeable chasm separated his culture from the academic theologians and from their partners in crime, the philosophers of the Arts faculty. He came to see the academic culture as the natural enemy of literature *(bonae litterae)* and became the great spokesman for the alternative.

In essence the humanist critique, as articulated by Erasmus, was threefold. The first criticism regarded content. The philosophers misdirected their attention to works about the physical universe to the neglect of human questions, and the theologians followed suit by a similar attention to metaphysics to the neglect of the literature most pertinent to their task—the Bible and the Fathers of the Church.

The second criticism regarded form or style of discourse. The ceaseless questioning, the compulsive analyzing, the corrosive disputing were inappropriate and counter-productive for sacred studies. The theologians, following methods learned in Arts, approached sacred texts in the wrong way.

The third criticism is perhaps the most comprehensive. The theologians did not live a "theological life." They made theology into a purely academic pursuit. They relied on the philosophy of Aristotle and other "scientific" thinkers and did not know "the philosophy of Christ," which besides having teachings was also a way of life. Erasmus preferred philosophers like Cicero in whom the connection between what is taught and how one lives is clear. He in effect correctly pointed out that with the birth of the academic style this aspect of philosophy prevalent in antiquity had been lost.

Luther, soon joined by others, launched the other challenge to academic theology. He directed his attack against the Arts faculty for teaching Aristotle's ethics, with its human doctrine that the practice of virtue leads to a righteous life, but especially against the theological faculties for thinking they had baptized that ethics and reconciled it with Paul's teaching on the utter gratuity of righteousness, grace alone. After his excommunication, as the theological establishment in most places began to take sides against him, he identified the theologians with the papists and saw the whole papal church corrupted to the core by this misbelief. Thus Luther attacked first of all the content of the Scholastics' teaching on the relationship between nature and grace. The great contest was between Luther's and the papists' doctrine of justification.

But the contest over style was just as profound and important as the contest over content. In Luther's "Disputation against Scholastic Theology," 1517, most of his theses deal with doctrines, only a few with method, but those few are crucial for revealing his rejection of the academic tradition in which he had been trained and in which he held a doctor's degree. In thesis 47, for instance, he said: "No syllogistic form is valid when applied to divine terms."[11] Even at this early date, then, Luther was creating a style of doing theology that, no matter what its component parts, fitted no sixteenth-century mold.

In 1521 in his long reply to Latomus, a theologian from the University of Louvain who had attacked him, Luther challenged academic method by adducing divine inspiration as the test for authenticity of teaching, and he presented the martyrdom of saints like Agnes, Lucy, and Anastasia to prove his point:

> My advice has been that a young man avoid scholastic philosophy and theology like the very death of his soul. . . . How was Christianity taught in the times of the martyrs when this philosophy and theology did not exist? How did Christ himself teach? St. Agnes was a theologian at the age of thirteen, likewise Lucy and Anastasia—from what were they taught? In all these hundreds of years up to the present, the courses at the universities have not produced, out of so many students, a single martyr or saint to prove that their instruction is right and pleasing to God. . . . I have the strongest doubts as to whether Thomas Aquinas is among the damned or the blessed . . . Thomas wrote a great deal of heresy and is responsible for the reign of Aristotle, the destroyer of godly doctrine.[12]

Despite their different approaches, both Erasmus and Luther agreed that one of the most deleterious results of the Scholastics' method was disenchantment. Through their ceaseless questions they analyzed Christian beliefs and dissected them into ever smaller units, cutting them down to human size. Scholastics professed to honor the inscrutable mystery that was at the heart of Christian faith, but by their style of discourse they were engaged in an enterprise that would explain the mystery away. For Erasmus their work was frigid. For Luther, ungodly.

Yet the universities, though criticized, remained hardy throughout the sixteenth century and would not experience real crises until later. In Europe in the sixteenth century, however, they began to undergo significant changes. "The Humanities" would, as mentioned, make inroads especially into the Arts faculty. The theological faculties in Protestant sectors of Europe would change notably from what they were before the Reformation and develop in ways different from their Catholic counterparts. Although the theological faculties in Catholic settings remained basically within the Scholastic framework developed since the thirteenth century, they too seemed to be increasingly sensitive to the humanists' critique, and they experienced in many places a new excitement generated by the emergence of great masters in the Thomistic tradition like Francisco de Vitoria in Salamanca and Thomas De Vio (Cajetan) in Padua and Rome.

A sign of the university's vitality in the sixteenth century is that precisely at that moment this preeminently European institution took its first steps toward an international presence that would be fully realized only in the twentieth century. In 1532 the papacy granted full university status, with all the privileges enjoyed by the Universities of Salamanca and Alcalá, to the school that members of the Dominican order had opened a few years earlier on the island of Hispaniola, the present-day Haiti and Dominican Republic. Some twenty years later universities were founded by royal authority in Lima and Mexico City. Others followed in Spanish and Portuguese America. In 1585 the Jesuits opened a school in Macau, just outside imperial China, that soon developed into a university. In 1636 the Puritans in Massachusetts Bay founded a school, soon to be known as Harvard, that, though it long eschewed the title university, from the beginning taught "higher subjects." Moreover, in Europe itself between 1500 and 1650 almost a hundred new institutions were founded that, with some stretching, can be categorized as universities, about thirty under Protestant aegis and the rest under Catholic.

When the bishops finally assembled at Trent in 1545, they came to realize that they had two tasks, not altogether distinct from each other. The first was to respond to the Protestants, especially Luther, on doctrinal questions and then to address the issue that had nagged the later Middle Ages and been made imperative by Luther, "the reform of the church." To address these tasks they knew they needed professional help, so they assembled a group of "experts," theologians and canonists trained in the universities.

The council would drag on, with two long intermissions, for the next eighteen years. It was a complicated event that, even after the masterly scholarship on it by Hubert Jedin and his disciples, still remains opaque to most people and the victim of centuries of propaganda, negative and positive. The bishops were the key players, of course, but the documents they produced were first hammered out by experts from culture two.

No matter how one judges the eventual outcome, the council displayed from the beginning a determination to face the issues before it and to listen to arguments. This is true despite the confusion that often raged in the debates and the wide variety of viewpoints that emerged—and that were later submerged in both the Catholic and the Protestant historiography. Although this determination can hardly be attributed just to the theologians and canonists, as a characteristic of culture two it fits their profile. The council, no doubt, operated in a conservative framework. It accepted without discussion what members for the most part believed to be traditional practices and beliefs, and it accepted, besides, the basic validity of the approaches to these issues common in the universities of the era. It did not, however, adopt the knee-jerk, negative reaction to issues often attributed to it.

Regarding doctrine the bishops relatively soon came to realize that, even though there was much confusion about Luther's teaching, justification was the key issue. Under the influence of Aristotle Catholics were accused of holding a Pelagian position, that is, by force of their "works" believing in effect that they could save themselves, perhaps with a little help from grace; or they might by their works merit the needed grace, thus forcing God's hand. It was a problem as old as the fifth century, resurrected now in an urgent form by Luther and others. Was Luther right? If not, what was the Catholic position?

Beginning in the spring of 1546 the theologians labored with the bishops for seven months on the justification decree. Rather than merely refute and reject what were deemed Luther's errors, the bishops, in tandem with the theologians, decided to make a full presentation on the positive side of what the true doctrine was. The theologians researched the writings of theologians from the past and examined the decrees of previous councils, including the recently rediscovered documents from the second Council of Orange, 529, that sided so decisively with Augustine's position on the utter gratuity and absolute necessity of grace for salvation. Although the theologians were not always well informed about Luther's position and viewed him with a hostile eye, their investigation into the problem was searching. They looked at the evidence.

The decree is the result of a corporate effort. The academics, for all their supposedly inveterate contentiousness, were by virtue of their academic positions used to working together. The universities required for their well-being as corporate enterprises the cooperation of all involved in them. In the sixteenth century the masters at Paris spent seemingly countless hours per week or per month in meetings with their peers. In 1523 members of the theological faculty there met 101 times (a record probably rarely bested even in universities today). The decree on justification at Trent is an example of the results that cooperation among academics could produce.

The decree consists of sixteen sections called chapters, followed by thirty-three brief canons. The chapters are an exposition of "the Catholic doctrine on justification," the canons are a sort of mirror reverse-image, rejections of false opinions on the subject. In English translation the whole decree runs about eleven pages of small print. Contrary to what might be expected, the chapters fairly effectively avoid using the technical language "of the schools." In the early weeks of the council, the bishops had decided to formulate their decisions as much as possible in the language of Scripture and the Fathers of the Church, and during the first period, 1545–1547, when the decree on justification was put together, they were fairly successful in adhering to this position.

Although earlier at the Council of Florence, 1437–1439, the bishops had arrived at a similar decision in order to accommodate bishops and theologians from Byzantium, who had no use for Scholastic method and discourse, at Trent the humanists' views on the matter, now long in circulation especially in southern Europe, help account for it. Humanist influence at the council was strongest during this period. The chapters are in fact not without a certain eloquence, which once again indicates that even in this century of bitter altercations between cultures two and three the lines of demarcation were not rigid. Later in the council, the bishops were less successful in avoiding Scholastic categories, especially when dealing with the sacraments, which constitute the great bulk of the council's doctrinal decrees. Even in the canons on justification the language is more redolent of culture two than it is in the chapters. For the chapters, however, the following sentence is typical: "Thus our own personal justice is not established as something coming from us, nor is the justice of God disregarded or rejected; what is called our justice, because we are justified by its abiding in us, is that same justice of God, in that it is imparted to us by God through the merits of Christ."

If in language the chapters on justification do not provide a neat counterpoint to humanistic culture, the council's pursuit of the issue down to the minutest detail runs against the instincts of that culture to remain on the level of general principle. The humanist ideal, almost certainly unrealizable in the heated doctrinal atmosphere of the day, would be to insist on a few basic and absolutely necessary truths and not countenance the production of an eleven-page menu of their ramifications and consequences.

Luther died the year before the decree was finished. The more influential of the theologians at the council like Gerolamo Seripando took seriously Luther's challenge of "works-righteousness," and they succeeded at every step in infusing into the decree strong doses of the doctrine of the gratuity of grace, while making it clear that the gratuity did not deprive human beings of some responsibility in their salvation. Ostensibly a rejection of Luther's teaching, was the decree on some deep level compatible with it? In recent decades some scholars have effectively argued that it was. But surely in its form, in its style, Trent's decree does not conform to Luther's utterances in his more prophetic moments.

The beauty of the chapters on justification lies in the patient, step-by-step development of the basic insights that guide them. Each chapter is a coherent unit, yet the chapters build to the coherence of the whole decree. In the process qualifications and distinctions are made, so that even with a relatively nontechnical vocabulary terms emerge fairly well defined. Once certain "first principles" are accepted, the decree makes sense. It holds together. It satisfies the mind. One of the "first principles," however, was the Scholastics', especially the Thomists', fundamentally optimistic assessment of "natures," including human nature. Even amid repeated references to sin and human impotence that assessment frequently surfaces. At least in that important regard, the decree is incompatible with Luther. But there is another aspect in which it also significantly differs from him.

"At the same moment saint and sinner"—*simul justus et peccator.* Thus Luther. Yes and yes, he asserted, seemingly without qualification. But grace and sin, reply the theologians, cannot (in a logical world) exist simultaneously in the same person any more than a pigment can be white and black at the same time. Luther's discourse is psychological and relational, the theologians at Trent logical and metaphysical. Luther glories in the paradox, the theologians are puzzled or even repelled by it. The decree of Trent was the scholars' solution to Luther's anguished cry. Wittgenstein's lion had been speaking. They responded to the lion not in his language but in theirs.

Moreover, although the decree on justification can be intellectually satisfying within its context, it packs no punch. It is measured. It is concerned not to overstate the case one way or the other and concerned to forestall possible misunderstandings. No slogan, therefore, can capture it, nor would culture two stoop to using one. "Faith alone," said Luther. Not quite, said Trent. "Grace alone," said Luther. Not quite, said Trent again. Trent by virtue of being Trent produced no sound bite to rival Luther's "justification by faith alone." By default others produced the sound bites, which usually badly distorted the message the decree wanted to get across. The rhetorical weaknesses of the style of culture two could hardly be better exemplified than here.

Luther did not live by slogans alone. Far from it. Early on in "Freedom of the Christian" he explained at length his teaching on justification, and he carried on learned discourse and disputation with his peers. He was himself a university professor. Other Protestants carried on similarly learned discourses on the issue, and many held similar academic positions. Lutheranism itself would by the seventeenth century slip into a Scholastic phase. Nonetheless, Luther as prophet, standing alone because he could do no other, asserting, manifests a culture quite different from the corporate and considered culture manifested in the Tridentine decree on justification.

The measured approach manifested itself in other issues in which the council, contrary to what is commonly thought, showed remarkable restraint. Justification was, yes, the central issue, yet some others, though they might seem secondary, were in fact much more palpable and visible, much more immediate to the life of the ordinary Christian, much more divisive on the day-to-day level. One of these issues was the language of the mass. Luther had early on put the service into German, and other Reformers later put their services into their respective vernaculars. Before the Reformation even Erasmus, the great Latin stylist, had advocated more use of the vernacular in the liturgy.

The council had to take up the issue. It did not do so until near the end, 1562. By that time, forty years after Luther's action, Protestants had made the vernacular a symbol and a rallying cry for the Reformation. Catholics, in reaction, had done the same for the traditional Latin. By 1562, therefore, it would seem almost inevitable that the council would ratify and insist upon the status quo. It did not. It treated this volatile issue in a single sentence in one of the chapters: "it has not been deemed advisable [to decree] that the mass be everywhere celebrated in the vernacular." In the canon pertaining to this chapter, the council repeats the same idea: "[it is wrong to maintain] that the mass be celebrated only in the vernacular."[13] In other words, Latin was legitimate, though not mandatory. The heat of battle outside the council prevented any hearing for the decision.

Another inflamed issue was the celibacy of the clergy. All Protestants condemned and had abandoned it. The council, once again, did not take up the matter until 1562. It was debated, with some theologians maintaining that celibacy was a tradition going back to apostolic times and hence not open to change. The council finally issued two canons dealing with the issue.[14] Though the canons obliquely support the discipline of celibacy, the language is careful and cautious, the language of professionals threading their way through difficult and disputed terrain. It was a decision of Pope Pius V after the council that finally settled the issue in favor of obligatory celibacy.

Besides dealing with Protestant teachings and practical matters like celibacy and the language of the liturgy, the council also had the task of reforming the church. In sheer quantity the reform decrees fill more pages than those dealing with doctrine. Although the immediate impetus that put reform on the agenda of the council was the crisis Luther set off, the reform decrees of Trent are not so much a counterpoint to Luther or Protestants as implementation of an agenda implicit in the traditional canons of the church, which dealt principally with the duties incumbent upon holders of ecclesiastical offices, especially bishoprics. For the bishops at Trent "reform of the church" meant reform especially of the episcopacy and then the pastorate through the enforcement of normative clerical discipline as handed down in canon law.

This meant that another university discipline, law, came heavily into play at Trent. In January 1521, when the bull excommunicating him went into force, Luther publicly burned along with it a book of canon law, his act of defiance against the church that had got lost in man-made laws and used them to terrorize Christians. The council paid no attention to Luther's rejection of the canons but simply as a matter of course based its reform on updating and implementing them, especially by the application of more severe penalties for disregarding them. To the bishops' credit, they directed some of the most severe penalties against themselves. The net result, in any case, was that the reform decrees of Trent can be read as a case study in surveillance and punishment.

If the legal profession stands for order, it consequently stands against violations of the order codified in the laws. In its culture two form it shares with theology the same propensity to tie up all loose ends and to close avenues of escape that violators might use. This propensity is manifest in the large number of canons the council issued "on reform" *(de reformatione),* in which the language is terse and technical, aimed at eliminating any ambiguity that could be used as a loophole.

The bishops knew that to accomplish their goals, such as insisting that bishops reside in their dioceses and perform their traditional duties, exhortations would not do the job. Erasmus criticized the tendency to prescribe remedies for every circumstance, and Luther held in contempt the swarm of canonists who had substituted their laws for the Gospel. But the bishops of Trent were convinced that all escape-hatches had to be shut tight if long-standing and deeply imbedded violations were to be eliminated, and they knew no better way to effect their goal than to put teeth in ancient traditions. They thus took on a reforming task, but they were not prophetic reformers. They moved within the conventions they knew. Their aim was not to change the system but to make it work.

The Resiliency of the Institution and Its Style

Even in the early seventeenth century the contours of culture two that had emerged in the High Middle Ages still seemed basically secure. The number of universities was expanding and their prestige remained high. Despite attacks on the methods and style of learning fostered in them, the basic presuppositions of their discourse remained fairly well intact. Profound changes were, however, already under way for both the institution and the discourse of culture two.

Athens and Jerusalem. The theological enterprise of the medieval university was centered on the relationship between faith and reason, that is, the Bible and Aristotle. The relationship could also be expressed, however, as one between two faiths—faith in the authority of the Bible and faith in the authority of Aristotle (and other ancient writers like Ptolemy). Aspects of this latter faith weakened and then crumbled in the seventeenth century. The aspect that first and most ostensibly suffered was not the ethics and the logic that Luther had attacked but "natural philosophy." Copernicus had led the way in the sixteenth century, but Galileo, Newton, Harvey, and numerous others in the seventeenth put investigation of the physical world on a basis that would leave behind Aristotle and other members of the "School of Athens" as not much more than historical curiosities. The quest of culture two was now the quest for hard data.

With faith in the ancients' analysis of the physical world shaken, faith in their metaphysical categories could not be unaffected. The conclusions about the way the metaphysical world worked that Aristotle and others had self-assuredly proffered as certain and sure were now up for questioning in a way they had never been in the Middle Ages. If those conclusions were not true, of what can we be certain? Descartes' search for certitude is of a piece with this situation. It put philosophy (in its contemporary sense of a specific discipline) on a new course. It changed much of the language and many of the presuppositions of academic discourse, but it did not displace the questioning that constituted its center.

Meanwhile, the university itself began to change and to assume a different and eventually more modest role in society. By the seventeenth century the *studia humanitatis* had secured space and prestige for themselves in the universities. Thus humanist critique of Scholastic learning had important repercussions for the culture of the university, though they manifested themselves differently in different countries. No doubt, however, as Marc Fumaroli has shown, the seventeenth century was not only the age of new sciences but "the age of eloquence" as well. The primacy given to the study of literature and the esteem for the ability to express one's thoughts with grace and persuasion marked a new, pan-European ideal.

Scientists were as proud of their ability to speak well as they were of their scientific achievements. When in the mid-eighteenth century Georges Buffon was elected to the Académie française, he spoke not on science but on style, to no one's surprise. Principally responsible for this dramatic shift in cultural values were the humanistic "secondary" schools in which boys who wanted to be truly educated enrolled in great numbers, but literature had also entered the stronghold of culture two and was doing well there. At Cambridge in the early seventeenth century Seneca, Cicero, Quintilian, Juvenal, Persius, Terence, Sallust, Ovid, and Martial formed an important part of a four-year curriculum. This new emphasis meant less attention to "natural philosophy," however, just at the time when the great scientific breakthroughs were occurring. If the universities seemed to be riding high at the beginning of the seventeenth century, by the middle of it the unquestioned dominance they had enjoyed in scientific and professional training was weakening.

The religious divisions, moreover, were taking their toll. The universities of the Middle Ages had a Christian character in that they were institutions in a society in which Christianity was a pervasive fact of life, taken for granted. But in the sixteenth century the universities became, to a greater or lesser degree, confessional institutions. In Geneva no student was admitted to study any discipline before signing a profession of faith. Lutheran universities required adherence to the Augsburg Confession. In Oxford and Cambridge from 1559 until 1871 all members of the university had to adhere to the Articles of the Church of England. Although Italian universities remained relatively tolerant, inquisitions and the governments in other Catholic territories tried to make sure no heretics appeared on the threshold of any university under their jurisdiction. This meant that the lively international character of the medieval university and the exchange of ideas it implied underwent some curtailment, and it obviously meant as well a muzzle on inquiry that might lead beyond the boundaries of the prevailing orthodoxy.

Universities also came into competition with other institutions whose curriculum and aims overlapped theirs. The Arts college directly competed with the now widespread humanistic schools, whose students came from approximately the same age group and whose curricula to a fairly large extent now overlapped. Seminaries had appeared in both Catholic and Protestant territories, with often an embryonic semi-university structure. Many seminary students did not go on to careers in ministry. Meanwhile, other new institutions that provided specialized, often highly practical training in subjects sometimes related to the traditional university curriculum began to spring up and have considerable success. Among them were, for instance, specialized schools in surgery (The Hague, 1637; Paris, 1724), engineering (Moscow, 1712), oriental languages (Naples, 1732), and commerce (Hamburg, 1768). These institutions seemed to say that the university was not a place where new disciplines were welcome and could evolve.

Just as important as these new schools was the rise in the seventeenth and eighteenth centuries of more informal institutions, like the salons of aristocratic women where the learned found patrons and a congenial atmosphere. Even more important were "academies" where men of letters and men of science gathered in a less structured and more flexible environment than the university, an environment that did not entail the time-consuming distraction of teaching students. As early as 1560 a physician named Giambattista della Porta founded an academy in Naples. The purpose was to bring together men who knew "anything that was curious," but membership was in fact restricted to those who had made a new discovery or observation of something in nature. This convergence of the learned led to important publications, in this instance to della Porta's twenty-volume work entitled *Natural Magic*, 1589.

By the seventeenth century academies had gained great momentum in northern Europe, where monarchs were often their patrons or founders. In 1635 Richelieu created the Académie française for the study of the French language. In 1666 Colbert created the Académie des sciences and the next year the Académie d'architecture. In 1662 a group of scientists and mathematicians in England obtained a charter from the king establishing themselves as the Royal Society of London for the Advancement of Natural Knowledge. They encouraged the testing of theories by experiments. The venue for asking the questions that really mattered and for carrying through on the answers had shifted away from the universities, but that basic enterprise remained the same.

In 1744 Benjamin Franklin was the principal founder in Philadelphia of the American Philosophical Society "for the promotion of useful knowledge," which meant, among other things, knowledge about "all new-discovered Plants, Herbs, Trees, and Roots, etc. Methods of Propagating them and making such as are useful. . . . All new Arts, Trades, Manufactures, etc., that may be proposed or thought of . . . And all philosophical Experiments that let Light into the Nature of Things, tend to increase the Power of Man over Matter, and multiply the Conveniences or Pleasures of Life."[15] In 1780 the legislature of the Commonwealth of Massachusetts passed an act incorporating the American Academy of Arts and Sciences, founded for similar purposes. Both organizations have enjoyed a continuous existence since their founding and are the two oldest learned societies in the United States.

With the emergence of learned societies came the emergence of what would develop into learned journals. In 1665 the Royal Society of London began a long series of publications entitled *Philosophical Transactions* that contained papers presented to the society, letters from abroad, and reviews of books. Other academies began to do the same. The American Philosophical Society published in 1771 the first number of its *Transactions.* The genre caught on fast. Not all these series and journals sprang out of academies. In 1701, for instance, the Jesuits launched their *Journal de Trévoux* to promote the study of the "history of sciences and the arts." In the creation and early development of the genre, however, the universities played no significant role.

The confessional identity that universities to a greater or lesser degree had assumed in the sixteenth century diminished their reputation in the eighteenth. In enlightened circles faith in Aristotle was long gone, but now faith in Christianity disintegrated as well. Universities were increasingly depicted as clerically dominated institutions, which by definition meant retrograde. The fear of such domination was more widespread and virulent on the Continent than in England or North America, but it was not unknown in those places. In view of the founding of King's College in New York, now Columbia University, the prominent journal *The Independent Reflector* pleaded in 1753 that the officers and students be free to attend any Protestant church and that no theology be taught: "Let not the seat of literature, the abode of the Muses, and the nurse of science, be transformed into a cloister of bigots, a habitation of superstition, a nursery of ghostly tyranny, a school of rabbinical jargon. The legislator alone should have direction of so important an establishment."[16] The last sentence was a harbinger, moreover, of the growing role governments would begin to play in higher education.

By the late eighteenth century, then, universities were heavily criticized for being out of touch, for producing work-shy pedants, and for being oblivious to the intrinsic relationship between education and a successful career. Research, open discussion of ideas, experimental science, the dissemination of new discoveries—this was the function of the academies. It was in academies that the probing style of discourse proper to culture two was to be found. Especially on the Continent thinkers promoted the idea that the universities were stuffy institutions, too rigid for the *hommes libres* of the Enlightenment whose eyes were fixed on the future, not on the past—Voltaire never held a university position, nor did he even hold a university degree. By the beginning of the nineteenth century in France and a few other places the very survival of universities was an open question.

But the institution showed itself to be remarkably resilient. There is no simple explanation for the resurgence of the university and of its transformation into the institutions we know today, institutions that in their ethos and drive, despite immense differences, more closely resemble their medieval antecedents than they do the universities of the immediately preceding era. No doubt, the firm and rational structures the university created for itself in its inception served it well. But the founding of the University of Berlin in 1810 is surely a landmark for its later history; by the second half of the century it had become the unquestioned model for educational reformers in the United States and Japan, and then for other countries as well. Almost from its founding it began to develop into an institution where research and the advancement of knowledge were the professed goals and enjoyed unquestioned primacy. There were more than forty other universities in the German states, a far larger concentration than in any other part of Europe. This was the matrix, or even network, that helped the new model spread. The "mandarin" professor, as critics designated the type, replaced the genial "Mr. Chips," who chatted his life away in the company of his students.

The university had, therefore, a new mission: its goal was now not simply the transmission of knowledge but the advancement of it. That the physical sciences "advanced" was taken for granted by the time of the Enlightenment, but in the new order of things so did the Humanities, that is, the disciplines traditionally associated with culture three. *Wissenschaft* in this model was dynamic and in all fields. At Berlin Leopold von Ranke had early in the century codified the ideal for the study of history, which began to replace rhetoric and philosophy as the unifying method in a variety of disciplines.

In the long run this development would mean the eventual disenfranchising of the learned amateur and the dilettante, acceptable though such persons had been even in many academies of the previous century. They would be replaced by the professional, trained in "scientific" methods and publicly certified with a Ph.D. That degree would gradually become the unquestioned prerequisite, waived under only the most extraordinary circumstances, for acceptance in the world of learning. It would become the unquestioned prerequisite for publishing in learned journals and for admittance to deliberations of learned societies. It would be required for employment in think tanks and laboratories owned, operated, and funded by business, industry, government, and special-interest groups. It could be earned only in a university. The degree, especially in the exalted form of the Ph.D, had staged a tremendous comeback as central symbol for culture two.

In the United States intellectually gifted and ambitious young men soon learned about what was happening in Germany, and they took advantage of it. They realized that "the colleges" of their own country provided no training at an advanced level, or at least no training that could compare with the rigor and depth that had become the norm abroad. The cultivation and advancement of *Wissenschaft* was not what these institutions were about. When in 1861 Yale conferred the first American Ph.D, it signaled the beginning of a great shift in North American education.

This was the stimulus for the creation in North America of a new entity, the Graduate School of Arts and Sciences, in which history, literature, and other "humanities" would be studied "scientifically." In the United States "the college" as such, the "alma mater" with its powerful rituals of sports and other forms of bonding, proved too emotionally sturdy to allow itself to be transformed into the German model. The solution was the addition of a superstructure, the Graduate School. Since the modern undergraduate college—"the Arts college"—retained at least in theory some of the aims and ideals of the humanist tradition, the result was the well-recognized and unresolved tension in American education between the supposedly student-centered and more generalist aims of "the college," and the specialized, technical, and research aims of the graduate school. In this situation undergraduate and graduate education sometimes became partners, sometimes competitors, sometimes enemies, sometimes strangers passing in the night—cultures two and three.

Meanwhile, training in the professions began to move back to the universities, which created schools or departments that replicated what some of the independent institutions founded in the eighteenth century did—schools of engineering, for instance, and of agriculture. Abraham Lincoln never went to law school, and in the nineteenth century many doctors of medicine never went to medical school. The universities began insisting, however, that only professional programs that led to a degree distinguished the professional from the charlatan—and they eventually insisted on this for architects, dentists, nurses, teachers. They insisted on it for businessmen, painters, sculptors, musicians, and, among others, hotel managers.

Some universities even had room for theology—or Divinity, as it was generally called in Protestant America. Nowhere was the establishment of Divinity more determinedly and professedly undertaken than at the new University of Chicago late in the nineteenth century, when the president, William Rainey Harper, and the university's chief benefactor, John D. Rockefeller, both devout Baptists, saw to it that the Divinity School was the first professional program put into operation in the university. Rockefeller and Harper hoped the Divinity School would be an integrating force on the campus, but in the ever more sprawling and decentered institution that universities were becoming, no discipline or department, it would seem, could fulfill such a hope.

At the end of World War II the GI Bill of Rights that provided a university education virtually cost-free to any veteran caused enormous expansion, making the universities even more complex. A "college education" became understood as the indispensable requirement for getting a "decent job." In this situation the vast majority of students entered the university in the hope of bettering their social and economic prospects rather than for love of *Wissenschaft.* To an unprecedented degree universities became agents on a broad scale of upward social mobility. They had evolved in every conceivable way into success-oriented institutions.

Success in scholarship and research is of a piece with this orientation. Despite the multiplicity of its scopes and promises, universities still claimed to exist for the pursuit of truth. *Veritas* is the single word on the seal of Harvard University, a change from the earlier *Veritas Christo et ecclesiae.* Research became the byword of the enterprise and its most revered aspect. It was a good in itself, having nothing directly to do with the researcher's moral improvement or with the betterment of society. Good teaching was important, but success in research was what was rewarded. This was true even for theology. When the Harvard Divinity School was reorganized in the early twentieth century, the president of the university, Charles Eliot, promised that the result would be "a broad School of Scientific Theology and independent research."[17] Teachers in both Protestant and Catholic seminaries in North America were gradually required to hold a Ph.D, a research degree—and then "to publish."

The publications that academic research has produced look not at all like the *summae* and the *quaestiones disputatae* of the medieval academics. They are structured altogether differently—yet the fact is that like these earlier works they are structured and ordered. Their vocabulary is different—yet in both cases it strives to be technical and precise, unambiguous and objective. The syllogism in its naked form has disappeared from the pages—yet sound, dispassionate argument is what is prized and the alternative not tolerated. Although Aristotle and the Bible are no longer the database, the footnote indicates what the new databases are. The disputation is gone as an academic exercise, but research goes nowhere without probing, reviewing, refining, and in part repudiating the findings of one's peers. To probe beyond the status quo is the essence of culture two and the source and expression of its dynamism. Why, otherwise, do lectures always end the same way: "Are there any questions?"

Culture two is not fond of paradox, yet paradox is perhaps the best way of describing what has happened to the style of discourse characteristic of it. The more its style has changed, the more it has remained the same.

CULTURE THREE

Poetry, Rhetoric, and the Common Good

EARLY IN Bertolucci's movie *The Last Emperor,* the story of Pu Yi from his infancy in the Forbidden City through his imprisonment under the Communist regime until his death in 1967, Reginald Johnston is hired by court officials to tutor the adolescent emperor in Western ways. The story is true, told by Johnston himself in his autobiographical recollection *Twilight in the Forbidden City.* In the movie, when Johnston talks to his young charge about the education he is to receive, he describes "a gentleman" as a person who says what he means and means what he says. A gentleman has at his command words that accurately convey his meaning, and he possesses the upright character that ensures he will stand by his words.

Johnston through Bertolucci captured a central tenet of a value system remarkable for its tenacity and resilience in the long journey from ancient Athens to the present—or at least almost to the present. In Athens by the fourth century B.C. this ideal had already been translated into a curriculum and, more important, the purpose of the training and the profile of "the ideal graduate" set forth, from which there would be remarkably little deviation. True, this culture achieved a sharpened identity for itself in the Renaissance in confrontation with the now fully established culture of the universities, yet even then it replayed many of the themes already articulated in the Roman Empire into which Christianity was born.

Athens and Rome

Until the fifth century B.C., Hellenic education had been based almost exclusively on poetry, which meant above all on Homer. The ideals held up for emulation were those of the noble warrior—bravery, loyalty, adaptability to the changing fortunes of war, virtuosity in song and sport, deference to the gods, and refinement of manners. By the time of Pericles they badly needed refashioning and supplementing. The hero in Athenian democracy was now the good citizen who contributed to the public weal. The ability to speak effectively on public issues took precedence over the ability to spin great yarns, and it began virtually to define success in the polis. Even more urgent, Athens had no lawyer class, so each citizen had to be able to argue his own case should he be hauled into court.

Already by the time of Solon in the sixth century, the traditional study of the poets began to entail teaching reading and writing, which would eventually develop into a systematic study of grammar, especially under the influence of the Sophists. The transition from a warrior to a more literary culture was, therefore, under way. It would lead in the fifth century to the production of an extensive corpus of masterpieces astounding for their range and aesthetic sophistication. Self-conscious principles of composition were applied to tragedy, comedy, various poetic genres, history, oratory, and philosophical dialogue—Sophocles, Euripides, Demosthenes, Hesiod, Thucydides, Pindar, the list goes on. This body of work was the product of an amazing convergence of creative genius. Nothing like it had been known before.

Skill in speaking and arguing was among the abilities the Sophists professed to have, and in the new political situation of democracy it was the skill that was needed. They helped make the Athenians aware of the power of speech, just as they themselves had become aware of it. Gorgias, in one of the few passages that has come down from him, put the matter succinctly: "Speech is a great power, which achieves the most divine works by means of the smallest and least visible forms; for it can even put a stop to fear, remove grief, create joy, and increase pity."[1]

The pieces were falling into place for the creation of the second essential building block in what would become the humanistic program: after the foundation had been laid in poetry, the culmination came in rhetoric, which meant in this instance oratory. Although rhetoric would be applied to written genres, it meant first of all principles and techniques for an effective speech-performance. At least some of the Sophists were not insensitive to the ethical issues such a performance implied, but in this regard they were no match for Plato's Socrates, who took them on for it.

Isocrates, a younger contemporary of Plato, heard Plato's criticisms of a morally neutral approach to rhetoric. Though deeply influenced by the Sophists, he took pains to distinguish himself from them and from all other educators of his time, and he was particularly concerned to relate rhetoric to virtue and worthy causes. He opened his school about 390. In it he did not claim to teach rhetoric, probably because of the bad name Plato had given it. The art he taught was the art of Logos, the art of the Word.

For Isocrates the foundation upon which the art of the Word was built was still the study of the poets, not only for the "grammatical" aspect of the study that he believed put word to thought or, better, begot thought through the right word, but also because literature revealed the complexity of the human situation. It was precisely that complexity, not something that could be reduced to a neat philosophical formula, that leaders in society had to deal with. Plato aimed at Truth and looked down upon "opinion" and probability. Isocrates thought probability was what most decisions in life were based upon, and hence the leader had to have the knack of hitting upon what was probably the most viable course of action.

Plato would banish the poets for their immoral stories. The tradition represented by Isocrates would retain them, in a position of honor, but increasingly interpret them "allegorically," that is, probe for the deeper truth that lay under the surface. Indeed later, by the time the Stoics appeared on the scene, the grammarian's highest task was the moral interpretation of the text: under a veil of myth Homer and the others hid a moral message.

Concerned though Isocrates was with the ethical dimension of education, he did not believe like Plato that moral goodness could be taught. Instead he insisted that the study of poetry and the study of political discourse could stimulate and develop good qualities if they were already present in the student. At the end of his life he wrote *Antidosis,* a long speech in defense of his life and work. In it he says:

> I think that there never was and is not now an art that can instill virtue and justice into those of a depraved nature . . . but I do think people can become better and worthier if they are ambitious about speaking well, and if they are enamored of being able to persuade their hearers. . . . It is not possible that a person choosing to speak or write speeches worthy of praise and honor will support unjust or petty causes or those concerned with private contracts; rather he will choose great and beautiful and humane subjects and those concerned with the common good. . . . And one who wishes to persuade others will not be negligent of his own virtue but will pay special attention to it.[2]

Plato opened his school, the Academy, a few years after Isocrates opened his. Whatever the similarities and differences between these two pivotal figures in their approaches to living and thinking, their schools help set patterns that would eventuate in two distinct ideals of education. Although both ideals took hold in the ancient Mediterranean world, sometimes in forms that made it difficult to differentiate one from the other, Isocrates' had by far the more immediate and widespread impact. With Alexander's conquests, the system he and his successors promoted spread broadly and would eventually conquer Rome itself.

Thus education in the Latin West, even more so than in the Greek East, was more exclusively grammatical and rhetorical, based almost entirely on a literary curriculum, with Latin authors eventually replacing their Greek equivalents. In conjunction with literature, almost as a subordinate part of it, subjects like arithmetic, music, and astronomy were also taught because the public person had to be able to engage a wide variety of subjects.

The education ended when students were in their late teens. Like its Greek counterpart, Roman education was radically "classical" in that it was pervaded by a sense that the corpus of great masterpieces at its core spoke as effectively to the present as to the past. It was also classical in that certain general ideals we still call classical were prominent in it—balance, harmony, proportion, moderation, and rationality. The ultimate goal was to produce a certain kind of person.

The high ideals that theorists like Cicero and Quintilian held up for Roman education were inculcated, it seems, indirectly, often pedantically, or not at all. Whatever the limitations of the system, it prepared youths of good families to be effective spokesmen for Roman political and commercial interests throughout the Mediterranean, to assume the duties of the many administrative offices that held this far-flung empire together, and to speak appropriately at ceremonial occasions great and small. Most important, whatever the limitations of the educational program, it was an essential part of the matrix that produced, as in Greece, an extraordinary number of literary masterpieces in a variety of genres.

Cicero remained the most prestigious Roman prose writer. While his orations were studied as models of their kind, his more reflective, even theoretical works, like his essays on friendship and old age, were more widely influential. None of his writings, however, was more important through the centuries than "On Public Responsibility" *(De officiis).* Among the patriots who pledged their "life, liberty and sacred honor" to pursue the American Revolution, John Adams was not alone in knowing some of these works almost by heart and in finding in them ideals he hoped would inspire citizens of the young republic.

Part of the appeal of these works was that they were "philosophical," meaning they dealt with ethical issues, especially as they touched on the common good and on civic responsibility. Cicero, extraordinarily well versed in the different philosophical schools of his day, even translated some of Plato into Latin and made the revealing statement, "I confess that whatever ability I have as an orator comes not from the workshop of the rhetoricians but from the spacious grounds of the Academy."[3]

In Cicero, then, cultures two and three seem to meet, their partnership manifest for all to see. For him eloquence was nothing other than wisdom put into appropriately persuasive expression. Two reservations need to be made, however, about this apparent harmony. The first, seemingly more superficial, concerns style. Although for Cicero the style of certain philosophers, especially Plato, was dignified and graceful, it did not convey the deep feeling that must animate the orator. It lacked ferocity, shrewdness, and pathos. It fell flat in the public forum.

The second reservation concerns the nature of the philosophy that Cicero admired. It included logic, dialectics, and rhetoric, but in contrast with medieval philosophy, it saw the first two as subordinate to rhetoric and its servants. It was also unlike medieval philosophy in that it had no intrinsic interest in natural philosophy except insofar as it filled in the orator's arsenal of examples and analogies. It was more centered on ethics and on political philosophy, on those branches of philosophy with a more direct bearing on life as it is lived with all its contingencies.

Cicero required a high moral level for citizens and especially for their leaders. He says in *De officiis:* "We are not born for ourselves alone. . . . Everything that the earth produces is created for our use, and we, too, as human beings are born for the sake of other human beings, that we might be able mutually to help one another; we ought therefore to take nature as our guide and contribute to the common good of humankind by reciprocal acts of kindness, by giving and receiving from one another, and thus by our skill, our industry, and our talents work to bind human society together in peace and harmony."[4]

For Cicero there was more to it than simply working together for an agreeable social order: "The duties prescribed by justice must be given precedence over everything else, including the pursuit of knowledge, for such duties concern the welfare of other human beings, and nothing ought to be more sacred in our eyes than that." Living a moral life required cherishing "the conviction that nothing but honesty and moral good deserves to be admired, wished for, or striven for." It required being ready to undertake actions "that are extremely arduous and laborious and fraught with danger both to life and to the many other goods that make life worth living."[5] It required a degree of self-sacrifice that Christians saw as consonant with what Christ required of his followers.

Christian Letters and Leaders

Why did the Christians of the early centuries decide to reconcile themselves with this culture and adapt elements from it for their purposes? The question is the equivalent of asking why Americans after the Declaration of Independence decided to continue to speak English. Just as those colonials could not step out of English, so Christians could not step out of a culture that a received and pervasive educational system had created over the course of several centuries or repudiate a body of literature that was all they knew. The analogy limps in that Christians clearly repudiated the gods of the poets and radically reshaped the this-worldliness of the pagan outlook, but even as they repudiated and reshaped they were so profoundly formed by this culture that it was part of their very souls. The analogy of "the spoils of Egypt" used by Augustine and others to justify their self-conscious appropriations misleadingly suggests that they could pick and choose at will from a reality that had to a large extent made them what they were.

A surprising number of the greatest figures in the Christian church were not only products of the literary education that every boy from a family of even somewhat moderate means received; they were also at one time or other teachers within it. In the East Origen, whose father, like Perpetua and Felicity, suffered martyrdom for his Christian belief under the emperor Septimius Severus, was a teacher of grammar (and thus of the pagan poets) before he opened his catechetical school at Alexandria. Gregory of Nyssa was a teacher of rhetoric before he became a monk and then a bishop. The letter by Basil, Gregory's older brother, endorsing for Christians the study of poets, a document important to the humanists of the Renaissance in justifying their enterprise, was but an articulation of widely held assumptions.

In the Latin West, five of the major Christian writers were teachers of rhetoric before their conversions—Tertullian, Cyprian, Arnobius, Lactantius, and, of course, Augustine, who taught rhetoric for thirteen years in Tagaste, Carthage, Rome, and Milan. Augustine's later revulsion at the emptiness of its content, *verba* without *res,* does not mean that he did not remain an accomplished rhetorician until his dying day. Of course, by assigning the pagan authors a role subordinate to the Bible, the Christian authors effected a profound change in the tradition while at the same time ensuring its continuance at an equally profound level.

Origen wrote in Greek, but, as indicated, he directly and indirectly influenced the West. In his homilies and his commentaries on the Bible we see the *grammaticus* still at work in ways that essentially determine their form and to some extent even their content. His procedure was the same exposition of the text that as a grammarian he used with the poets and other pagan authors. The word-for-word or passage-by-passage approach was the same and so were the techniques of interpretation for specific problems. As the *grammaticus* sat in his classroom commenting on Homer, so did Origen sit in the church commenting on the Bible. And so, later, would bishops in the West sit in their *cathedra* commenting on that same text, just as St. Bernard even later would sit in his abbot's chair delivering his homilies.

Good grammarian that Origen was, moreover, he, like his pagan counterparts in their study of Homer, searched for the most reliable versions of the biblical text upon which to base his remarks. That zeal for a correct text led him to pursue Hebrew and eventually construct his *Hexapla,* the first critical work on the Old Testament. When in the *Hexapla,* to give a quite specific example, he found a passage in the Septuagint, the standard Greek translation, but not in the original Hebrew, he marked it with an obelus; when there was a passage in the Hebrew but not in the Septuagint, he inserted an asterisk. The obelus and the asterisk were the critical signs used by the grammarians at Alexandria in their editions of Homer.

Origen had a profound reverence for the sacred text. Every part of it contained sublime mysteries, even when the surface meaning seemed pedestrian or even banal. "Observe each detail in what has been written," he says in a typical passage. "For, if one knows how to dig into the depth, he will find a treasure in the details, and perhaps also the precious jewels of the mysteries lie hidden where they are not esteemed."[6] To uncover the deeper meaning he turned to allegory, which not only was an unquestioned technique in the grammarian's tradition but by now had been sanctioned for the exegete through its use by Hellenized Jews like Aristobulus, Philo, and Paul.

While honoring the literal sense, Origen dug deeper for a spiritual sense. That sense saved the text from saying anything unworthy of God. As spiritual, it nourished and warmed the soul, turning it to God and to prayer. Apart from apologetics, fostering that turn was the main purpose of exegesis. In several ways, then, Origen interprets the Bible as if it were a book of poetry.

Typical is his comment on the verse from Genesis about Rebecca's coming to the well where she would meet Isaac's servant (24:15–16):

> Rebecca came to the wells daily; she drew water daily. . . . Do you think these are tales and that the Holy Spirit tells stories in the Scriptures? This is instruction for souls and spiritual teaching that instructs and teaches you to come daily to the wells of Scripture, to the waters of the Holy Spirit, and always to draw water and carry home a full vessel just as also holy Rebecca used to do. . . . Unless, therefore, you come daily to the wells, unless you daily draw water, not only will you not be able to give a drink to others, but you yourself also will suffer a thirst for the word of God.[7]

He goes on to give an almost mystical interpretation of the power of the Scriptural word: "All these things that are written are mysteries. Christ wishes to espouse you to himself. . . . Because, therefore, he wishes to espouse you to himself he dispatches to you his servant in advance. That servant is the prophetic word. Unless you have received it first, you cannot be married to Christ."[8]

The allegorical sense was multilayered. Origen probably took from Philo the theory that there were several levels of meaning to the text, and he introduced the idea of such levels into the Christian mainstream. As multilayered, the allegorical sense was remarkably fluid, so long as it conformed to basic Christian teachings. It was a flexible hermeneutic that allowed exegetes to say what they thought appropriate to audience and situation and also to bring the audience back to the few, great truths that should guide their lives. That is precisely what Origen does. Even for the practical aspects of the Christian life, he insisted in generic terms on living out one's inherent dignity and avoiding sin. Rather than moralize about sin and temptation, he exhorted his listeners to nourish their souls with the word of God. In staying on such general levels in both doctrine and the practice of the Christian life, Origen is consonant with a basic impulse of culture three.

Origen as *grammaticus* exemplified and very much helped establish basic approaches to the Bible that would characterize exegesis into the modern era. He also set the pattern that most preaching would take until the thirteenth century. Origen's homilies show unmistakable marks of rhetorical techniques, but the homily is quite different from the great orations, panegyrics, and funeral eulogies in which some of the Fathers were so proficient and which would be revived in the Renaissance. These latter were true speeches trying to make a single point. They had beginning, middle, and end, unlike the "formless form" of the homily that wandered wherever the next passage in the text took it and that ended when time ran out or the homilist tired. The sacred orator stood and gestured, hoped to arouse deep feeling, and used his voice in different intonations, inflections, and volume to do so. The homilist just commented on the text. Like a schoolmaster, he sat and, probably often enough, droned on.

Even Augustine, the great rhetorician, preached in what was basically the homiletic form. His conversion to Christianity really began when he listened to the homilies of Ambrose, bishop of Milan, who himself was influenced by Origen: "And when Ambrose lifted the veil of mystery and disclosed the spiritual meaning of texts that, taken literally, appeared to contain the most unlikely doctrines, I was not aggrieved by what he said, although I did not yet know whether it was true."[9] Later, as bishop himself, Augustine could do no better than follow Ambrose's example.

During the patristic era preaching and exegesis of the Scriptures were just two sides of the same coin, and in those two sides the "grammatical" or "poetic" aspects of culture three to a large extent determined how bishops would go about their work. There was, however, another dimension to the bishops' duties that was more closely related to the rhetorical aspects. It has been less noticed but is just as important. The profile of the "ideal graduate" of the rhetorical schools provided a blueprint for the bishops as *episkopoi,* that is, literally, as overseers or managers or governors. The profile for the *praefectus urbis,* the prefect of the city, revealed to the *praefectus ecclesiae,* the prefect of the church, how to conduct himself. It indicated the qualities he needed to carry out his duties as a civic notable in ways society had come to expect.

Pope Gregory the Great illustrates the point beautifully. Son of a Roman senator, he was prefect of the city of Rome before he became bishop of Rome in 590. Devout and austere to the point of spending several years in a monastery, he was respected for his integrity. Yet his election to the papacy in a particularly difficult time when Rome was threatened by the Lombards and seemed abandoned by the emperor in Constantinople was surely not unrelated to the success of his earlier political and diplomatic experience, for which his education had equipped him.

While bishops looked especially to the Pastoral Epistles of the New Testament for validation of their position and for a few guidelines as to their behavior—sober, of one wife, effective heads of their own households—they did not find there any indications of how to handle the responsibilities that especially by the fourth century challenged bishops as leaders of communities numbering thousands or tens of thousands of Christians. They did not find any precise indications as to how bishops should deal with each other and act collegially.

No matter how assiduously they read the New Testament, the bishops did not and could not find there the "course in management" they required for the duties that Constantine's recognition of Christianity had thrust upon them. Rhetorical education implicitly advertised itself to be precisely such a course. It taught the absolutely essential skills in writing and speaking that bishops needed to communicate with each other and with civic officials across the miles from Spain to Milan, from North Africa to Rome. The deliberative genre of oratory, the genre appropriate for winning consensus in a deliberative body for a course of action, implicitly suggested how to get people to work together for a common goal.

The bishops might insist that an unlettered Christian knew more true philosophy than the most learned pagan teacher, and they were struck with wonder that the Gospel was spread by ignorant fishermen. They gloried that Anthony, a farmer's son ignorant of Greek and Latin literature, could teach true wisdom to those who vaunted their sophistication. The bishops conveyed this praise of the power of ignorance and crude speech with all the erudition and eloquence their education had put at their disposal.

But this *paideia* claimed to do much more and had established the expectation that only its products were qualified to lead society—whether in Alexandria, Constantinople, Carthage, or Milan. Why in 373–374 did the Milanese by acclamation insist that Ambrose become their bishop? He knew no theology, had taken no part in church affairs, and, though from a Christian family, had not yet even been baptized. Jerome's typically sharp-tongued description dramatizes the event: "Yesterday a catechumen, today a bishop; yesterday in the amphitheater, today in church; in the evening at the circus, in the morning at the altar; formerly a fan of actors, now a consecrator of virgins."[10] Ambrose said of himself: "I was snatched for the priesthood out of law courts and high administrative office. I began to teach you what I had never learned."[11]

Ambrose, governor of Emilia-Liguria, had come to the cathedral to try to forestall the rioting expected to break out as the Milanese chose a new bishop. After he spoke for a long time urging deliberation and peace, just what officials were supposed to do in this often violent society, the cry broke out, "Ambrose, bishop!" Although Rufinus' account of the event does little justice to other factors such as the awe Ambrose's office itself would have inspired, it does mirror the results society expected from a good speech.

It was Ambrose's performance as eloquent governor, not a career in the church, that qualified him to be bishop. His later boldness in dealing with emperors, which would be held up for centuries as an ideal for ecclesiastics in their dealings with secular authorities who overstepped their bounds, can hardly be explained apart from the confident poise with which his education and former office had imbued him. He had appropriated from the Ciceronian ethos, it seems, the magnanimity and willingness to undertake arduous and dangerous courses of action when the common good called for it.

Ambrose's admiration for Cicero prompted him to write his own *De officiis.* He intended it primarily for his own clergy, some of whom would later become bishops, but also for a wider Christian audience. He surely wanted to demonstrate how the Christian ethos was better than anything "Athens" offered, yet even by the title that he adopted he fitted what he said into the patterns established by that very Athens. There are particulars that indicate how deeply the assumptions of Athens had sunk in. According to

Ambrose, for instance, after one's duties to God comes duty to one's country, *patria* (1.127). He is but echoing Cicero, who in his work by the same name put responsibility for one's country after duties "to the immortal gods," and then, as in Ambrose, responsibility for one's family, and finally for others. This is surely not a hierarchy of responsibilities found in the New Testament. "For God and country"—*Deo et patriae*—would in the modern era become a motto for schooling derived from the tradition of culture three.

In the book Ambrose also betrayed the little interest that the literary culture typically had shown for natural philosophy, which it deemed a distraction from more important things. "What is so misguided," he says, "as to spend time in the investigations of astronomy and geometry that [the philosophers] carry out, as well as measuring the great extent of the air and in trying to contain the heavens and the sea within numbers, which means leaving unstudied the causes of salvation and pursuing errors."[12] He could not have expressed his antipathy for the central discipline of culture two more sharply than when he observed, "God did not choose to save his people by using dialectics"—*Non in dialectica complacuit Deo salvum facere populum suum.*[13]

Those who passed through the schools of the rhetors were presumed not only to speak in a more refined and socially acceptable manner but also to have acquired a physical bearing that was dignified and inspiring of respect. They were even expected to have a countenance that reflected the wisdom that knew when to be grave and when to be in lighter humor, that knew when to tolerate missteps and when to intervene, that knew how in intervening to do so deftly. The exterior reflected the interior, an assumption surely behind Ambrose's insistence that his clergy convey even in their style of walking "an appearance of authority, a sense of serious purpose, an imprint of serene self-possession."[14] More deeply, the verbal decorum that the rhetoricians inculcated fostered not only a sense of what words or styles were appropriate for a given situation but, it was assumed, a sense of what was appropriate behavior in all the circumstances of life, including messy political or, as here, ecclesiastical imbroglios.

For bishops the civic aspects of their position went unquestioned. They almost inevitably and unawares accepted as a mode of their job description the public-servant model they had learned in school. In 368 Basil, already bishop of Caesarea, founded a large leper colony on the outskirts of the city. In a letter to an official he rather dismissed the accomplishment by saying he had done no more than any well-intentioned governor was expected to do. It is a telling remark. Good will toward one's city was a key virtue in the traditional *paideia.* As we will see, it was as builders that the bishops of the fourth century made their clearest statement of benevolence toward the city in which, from which, by which, and for whose good they had been elected. In the bishops of the patristic era, though they were perhaps more deeply motivated by their Christian faith, the ideals of culture three held fast a piece of their souls.

As the institutions and traditions of the Roman Empire weakened over the next centuries, the level of literacy and literary culture declined. The centers for instruction established under the aegis of the empire almost disappeared, resulting often in a clergy unable to read or understand the basic texts of their office and in a laity even worse off. For the most part only the monasteries or quasi-monastic institutions provided the leisure and isolation that would allow learning to continue amid the turmoil wracking society. The traditional organization of learning around progression from grammar to rhetoric, however, gradually disappeared. The trivium and quadrivium, already in the process of formulation in late antiquity, replaced it.

Outside Italy, the monks of Ireland and then England would be especially important for composing Latin hymns, excelling as illuminators of sacred texts, and copying important manuscripts. The texts of a surprising number of classical authors, particularly poets, were not only transmitted by them but continued to be known and read. In Alcuin's circle in the ninth century Horace, Lucretius, Ovid, Terence, Persius, Juvenal, and of course Virgil, by far the most important, were in circulation.

Virgil's popularity never flagged. Even the author of *Beowulf* probably knew him in some form. As in antiquity, grammar was studied primarily from the poets, and Virgil was the text for it par excellence. St. Odilo, the great abbot of Cluny in the first half of the eleventh century, knew the *Aeneid* so well that he could extemporaneously adapt lines from it to suit circumstances. The *Aeneid* was the primary text establishing Virgil's unchallenged authority, but his fourth *Eclogue,* interpreted as a veiled prophecy "among the Gentiles" of the coming of Christ, won him special deference.

No more resounding testimony to Virgil's supreme authority and to his influence on vernacular poetry exists than Dante's tribute in the opening canto of the *Commedia:* "You are my master. You are my author. From you alone I derived my fair style that wins me honor." Virgil, no other, was to lead Dante through the first half of his long journey to the godhead. "Lead on," Dante says to him at the end of that first canto. "So he moved on, and I behind."

The old authors survived. As verses from Dante indicate, they would have considerable influence on the development of vernacular literature. They also sparked a new Latin literature, modeled on the old, that developed sometimes in the most unlikely circumstances. In the late tenth century in the monastery of Gandersheim in Saxony a nun named Hrotswitha became the first dramatist to emerge in the West after the demise of the ancient classical theater. Writing in part in reaction to what she saw as the immorality of Terence, she composed plays that extolled Christian virtue and its superiority to anything the pagan world offered. Even as she reacted against Terence, she showed a profound acquaintance with him and imitated his elegance and grace of expression. Besides her six dramas, her most important and original works, she wrote eight poems of substantial length and other smaller works. In her monastery she had been solidly grounded in the trivium and quadrivium and had moved beyond them to familiarity with a considerable range of classical literature.

True, Gandersheim, a monastery founded for noble women and governed by them, cannot be taken as normative for the quality of learning in other monasteries, male or female. But it correctly suggests that in a relatively large number of circles the level of appropriation of culture three was, by the tenth or surely the eleventh century, high and resulted in literary creativity. The cathedral schools were developing, moreover, into training centers for service at court, whether episcopal or secular, and their program, drawing inspiration, it seems, from the Ciceronian tradition, aimed at producing young men who would be effective administrators and statesmen—eloquent, grave in manner, firmly grounded in virtue. The "civic" aspect of the program is intimated by the words of a cleric of Worms to his bishop in the early tenth century: "Divine providence, in foreseeing the necessity of installing you as the governor of our republic, has placed you at the apex of pastoral care in order that you may now translate into acts of public administration the things you have learned in private studies."[15]

In the first half of the twelfth century the promise of the preceding centuries reached a culmination in both vernacular and Latin literature. It was the time of the troubadours, but also the time of the great Cistercian abbots—Guerric of Igny, St. Aelred of Rievaulx, and St. Bernard himself. The Cistercians, recently founded, experienced a half-century of remarkable growth, owing in large measure to their remarkably learned and eloquent abbots. Aelred and Bernard were in their early twenties when they entered the monastery, and Guerric even older. They all had received their impressive educations, therefore, before they became monks, a sign of the high level of Latin literacy and literary accomplishment common by then in aristocratic families.

Aelred wrote his dialogue on "spiritual friendship" as a Christian adaptation of Cicero's *De amicitia,* much as Ambrose had done for the *De officiis.* He tells how as a youth he was "often deceived by what resembled friendship. Then, after some time, I acquired Cicero's famous book on friendship, and at once it seemed to me both useful in its weighty thoughts and pleasant in its agreeable eloquence." As his love for Scripture grew, he found that Cicero's book was not so attractive as it once was. Yet he constantly asked himself "whether by chance what I had learned from Cicero could be supported by the authority of Scripture." He implicitly managed a reconciliation, but what emerges most clearly from his pages is the great Cistercian theme of love. He says toward the end of the work:

> Is it not a certain share of blessedness so to love and be loved, so to help and be helped, and thus to fly higher, from the sweetness of brotherly charity to that more sublime splendor of divine love, and now to ascend the ladder of charity to the embrace of Christ himself, and then to descend by the same ladder to the love of one's neighbor, where one may sweetly rest? . . . But now the sun is setting, and we should end this conversation of ours. Do not doubt, then, that friendship proceeds from love. Indeed, whoever does not love himself, how can he love another, since he ought to order the love with which he loves his neighbor by its similarity to the love which makes him dear to himself?[16]

Bernard's masterpiece is his series of homilies on a love lyric, the Song of Solomon. In commenting on a piece of literature, he created another impressive piece of literature. "The text we are to study," Bernard says about the Song, "is the book of our experience. You must therefore turn attention inwards." The experience to which Bernard referred was the experience of conversion from sin and sadness to the joy and delight of love. The Song is about "the gift of holy love, the sacrament of endless union with God." The person meditating upon it is filled "with endless delight" because the Song celebrates the joy of the soul united with God: "Let those who are versed in this mystery of love revel in it; let all others burn with desire rather to experience it than to understand it. For it is not a melody that resounds abroad but the very music of the heart, not a trilling on the lips but an inward pulsing of delight, a harmony not of voices but of wills. It is not a tune you will hear in the streets; these notes do not sound where crowds assemble; only the singer hears it and the one to whom he sings—the lover and the beloved."[17]

As with Bernard's contemporaries, the vernacular poets of the courts, love was the theme of all themes. As Bernard's hermeneutical lens, love had the effect of almost turning the whole Bible into a love story. The exegete's task was to discover that message in the often coded way in which God delivered it. For its intimations of intimacy and its sometimes erotic overtones, there was nothing in patristic literature quite like what Bernard (and other Cistercians) produced. Yet what he produced is in the heritage of culture three, reworked and radically adapted. The same allegorical principles of interpretation are at work. In this instance, the patent eroticism of the Song gets transformed into something quite different. The Cistercians, like all poets, emphasized the delightful ambiguity of the texts that spoke to them. Whatever turned the monks to devotion was a legitimate interpretation, for that is what the Bible and the liturgical texts dependent upon it were written to accomplish—to enkindle love.

Unlike the sermons the Scholastics proposed in their *Artes praedicandi* that were tightly structured and moved from point to point and from proof to proof, Bernard's homilies, like a good poem, are going nowhere. He gets stuck on the opening verse of the Song, "He will kiss me with the kiss of his mouth." Bernard circles around the verse, he hovers over it. "The kiss"—for him its spiritual significance was inexhaustible. Bernard is interested not in proving that the kiss is significant, which he takes for granted, but in savoring it, in relishing it, in letting it refresh and delight his soul. He lingers. He cannot bring himself to move on.

The text, always pointing to love, yielded along the way multiple interpretations. In his second homily, Bernard explains the kiss of the beloved as a metaphor for the person of Christ and thus of the union in him of the human and divine natures. It is thus a metaphor of the Incarnation, in which the divine kissed the human and became united with it. He concludes the passage, however, with the words, "You seem to be in agreement with this explanation, but I should like you to listen to another."[18]

Guerric is no different. Commenting on a verse from Zechariah that was read in the Liturgical Hours for the day, he concludes, "Others may give what interpretations they will or can. . . . For myself I accept, venerate, and embrace whatever is in accord with the rule of faith and does not venture too far from the liturgical context." In commenting on the verse from the Song, "Your two breasts are like two fawns" (4.5), he unselfconsciously presses this approach to its limits. Taking "the bridegroom" of the text as usual as a coded designation for Christ, he says: "The Bridegroom himself has breasts better than wine. The Bridegroom, I say, has breasts, lest he should be lacking any one of all the duties and titles of loving kindness. He is father in virtue of creation or new birth that comes through grace, and also in virtue of the authority with which he instructs. He is mother, too, in the mildness of his affections, and a nurse because he is so attentive to the care such a duty imposes."[19]

The literature produced by the Cistercians had tremendous religious appeal. In a short time Bernard emerged as the most quoted

Christian author after Augustine, a distinction he retained well into the seventeenth century. He was referred to with reverence as “the devout Bernard” *(devotus Bernardus)* and as “the most holy abbot” *(sanctissimus abbas)*. Other authors were satisfied to rest their opinions upon his authority, even to the point of attributing to him their own thoughts and words to win acceptance. Bernard takes over from Beatrice in the final canto of the *Commedia* to lead Dante, through the Virgin, to his goal.

Luther approved of him. Because of the literary style of his writings, in the sixteenth and seventeenth centuries Bernard came to be known as “the last of the Fathers,” and Migne took his great edition of the *Patrologia latina* all the way up to the twelfth century, so as to include Bernard and his generation. “Last of the Fathers”—the designation is apt. Despite the differences, Bernard’s style and aims fit into the literary character of the Fathers’ enterprise. The traditions of poetry and rhetoric on which patristic theology most often and most characteristically lay found a new expression in Bernard and his colleagues.

Bernard died in 1153. He died just as a new theology was coming into being, a theology he sensed as the enemy of the tradition in which he stood. It is in this context that his fiercely intemperate attack on Abelard, “the knight errant of dialectics,” must be placed. Bernard seconded the judgment about Abelard made by William of St. Thierry, his friend and fellow Cistercian. The judgment portended a future beyond what either of them dreamed: “This is a new theology and a new theologian.”[20]

The very word *theology* now began to gain currency, gradually replacing the traditional “sacred doctrine,” a signal of a profound change. Sacred doctrine was moving into a new name, moving into culture two, moving into a classroom to become a full-fledged subject in a university curriculum. In that shift, preaching would emerge as one thing, being a theologian another. In the shift dialectic and the art of definition gained primacy over grammar/

rhetoric and the art of ambiguity. The art of linear thinking gained ascendancy over the art of rumination and of free association of images. Poetry ceded to logic.

The Renaissance

The thirteenth century has been described as the least literary of the centuries, a generalization that does not bear up under close scrutiny. It was, after all, the century of *Le Roman de la Rose* and Guido Cavalcanti. Dante had written *La vita nuova* years before it ended. But the emergence of the universities and their style of discourse is what especially grabs our attention. With literature as such virtually excluded from the university curriculum, it is not surprising that with time the literary tradition reasserted itself. Its profile was more sharply articulated than in antiquity because it now had an obtrusive alternative against which to measure itself and to formulate its ideals. We know the results of that articulation as Renaissance humanism, and, though it had remote and more proximate anticipations, we conventionally assign its beginnings to the mid-fourteenth century, to Petrarch. Aquinas died in 1274. Petrarch died exactly a century later, in 1374.

"When Petrarch besought his countrymen to close their Aristotle and open their Cicero," said R. R. Bolger almost a half-century ago, "he was most truly the Father of the Renaissance."[21] Even with all we now know about the first stirring of what led up to Petrarch and made him possible, Bolger's assessment still holds fairly well, especially if what we mean by Renaissance in this context is the outburst of literary creativity we associate with that period and especially the literary and educational movement known as humanism.

Petrarch—there were at least two sides to this complex man. He composed vernacular poetry of the highest merit, and his *Canzoniere* had great impact on the further development of poetry across Europe. In that regard he represents the astounding outburst of literary masterpieces that characterized the fourteenth century. Among the great geniuses of his day were not only Dante, of course, but also Boccaccio and Chaucer, who was himself influenced by the Italian geniuses.

Petrarch was also fascinated by the literary achievements of Roman antiquity and campaigned for their reinstatement, of course in the original Latin. It was this latter side of him that initiated the first steps in what would result in a fully deliberate and historically aware reconstruction of the classical *paideia,* that is, in the rebirth or renaissance of the program of literary education.

Two further aspects to Petrarch not only help establish his significance but also echo and articulate earlier traditions of culture three, giving them new currency in the fourteenth century. The first concerned language. What Petrarch saw as the jargon of the university teachers provided him with a contrast to the eloquence he deemed appropriate for human communication, not least of all because it was capable of motivating people to worthy goals: "It is one thing to know, another to love; one thing to understand, another to will. Aristotle teaches what virtue is, I do not deny that, but his lesson lacks the words that sting and set afire and urge toward love of virtue and hatred of vice or, at any rate, does not have enough of such power. Anybody who looks for that will find it in our Latin writers, especially in Cicero and Seneca, and, what may be astonishing to hear, in Horace, a poet somewhat rough in style but most pleasing in his maxims."[22]

That passage, from a work Petrarch composed late in life, can stand as a kind of manifesto for the campaign, sometimes feisty, that the most prominent of the Renaissance humanists—Petrarch, Lorenzo Valla, and Erasmus—would lead against what Petrarch called "the crazy and clamorous set of Scholastics."[23] It was a campaign against "Aristotle" both because of the barbarous style, according to the humanists, in which his works came down to us and because of the even worse style of his followers in the universities. It was a style that did not lead to the philosophical life. Humanists after Petrarch would have just as many negative things to say about "Aristotle," but for the most part they respected and utilized his works on logic and especially his *Poetics, Rhetoric, Politics,* and, *pace* Petrarch, his *Ethics,* works dealing with subjects congenial to culture three.

The second aspect of Petrarch's significance is related to the teaching of Aristotle's natural philosophy, which he criticized for its focus on the physical world, on "science," rather than on human beings and their deepest concerns. "What is the use," Petrarch said, "of knowing the nature of quadrupeds, fowls, fishes, and serpents and not knowing or even neglecting our own human nature, neglecting the purpose for which we are born, and whence and whitherto we travel."[24] The passage captures the turn to humanity that the humanists advocated—not a turn to humanity to the exclusion of divinity, as the nineteenth century often interpreted it, but a turn to humanity that would lead to its ultimate goal, God. The passage also suggests the formative dimension of the *studia humanitatis* ("the classics") that the school program of the humanists, once put in motion, entailed.

These two aspects of Petrarch's enterprise are in themselves unexceptional in culture three. What now imbued them with energy was the conviction that good style and concern for humane values had been lost or corrupted and had to be recovered and reestablished in their pristine form. The present was different from the past, discontinuous with it and all the worse for the discontinuity. Awareness of the difference gave the humanists a cause. It moved them to more assiduous study of the past, helped spur them to search more diligently and systematically for ancient writings that had disappeared, and motivated them to correct those that time and careless copying had vitiated. It helped bring into even stronger relief the gulf that many of them felt separated culture two from culture three. It would generate a self-conscious "rebirth of good letters" that included the educational philosophy imbedded in some of them.

By sheer force of his writings Petrarch won hearing for his ideas. Though of socially insignificant origins, he became a celebrated figure throughout Europe, especially in Italy, a status he did not at all disdain. In his achievement he of course does not stand alone, but he was, no doubt, the first powerful and widely heeded voice in the call *ad fontes*—"back to the sources," the genuine sources of culture and civility. He and those who believed as he did were catalysts for a reassertion of culture three that soon found grounding in public realities, as in chanceries, where the ability to formulate official documents in elegant Latin style became a prerequisite for holding office.

The humanists cultivated the literary genres appropriate to their enterprise. They produced no *summae* and no *quaestiones disputatae,* genres they despised. Petrarch as poet composed in both Italian and Latin. The *Canzoniere* become models for the genre, but with his Latin *Africa* he helped spark an enthusiasm for neo-Latin poetry. From the very beginning of the movement, therefore, poetry regained its honored and traditional place.

In 1345 Petrarch discovered in the cathedral library in Verona Cicero's letters to Atticus, which encouraged him to organize his own correspondence and helped revive epistolography as a distinctively humanist genre. The standard Latin edition of Erasmus' correspondence runs to eleven volumes and contains 3,141 letters. Such letters were often intended for an audience beyond the addressee. They were a way of communicating opinions on topics of the day and sometimes acted almost as book reviews of works published by contemporaries. They also told of personal successes or distress, sought to comfort the grieving, and tried to vindicate one's position on a given issue to the point of becoming a small treatise on it.

In 1444 Leonardo Bruni completed "*History of the Florentine People,* his greatest achievement but only one of his many historical works, all modeled on the masters from antiquity. Fascination with the past led humanists to cultivate the study of history in a way and to a degree not known since antiquity, and, indeed, a sense of the historical conditioning of language, ideas, and customs was characteristic of their approach to just about everything they discussed. This was an approach they found deplorably lacking in the academic establishment of their day.

Petrarch's *Secretum* is an imaginary dialogue between St. Augustine and Petrarch himself, based on classical and early Christian models, especially the *Confessions.* It is the first in what would become a genre especially cultivated by the humanists and particularly indicative of their culture. (Drama is its sibling, which somewhat later in England, Spain, and France boasted some of the world's greatest masters of the genre.)

In the dialogue the speakers sometimes seem to drift off the subject. They express different opinions, and they generally come to no clear resolution of them. The dialogue dramatizes the complexity of issues and the various perspectives that can be brought to bear on them. It suggests that probability is often as close as one can come to the truth or to the best course of action.

Erasmus' *Colloquies* are the most famous of the Renaissance dialogues. Many of them make a serious point through humor. Although Erasmus is usually clear about which opinion he favors, he still captures the essential points of the dialogue as a genre—a seemingly meandering exploration of competing opinions and a reluctance to prescribe pat solutions. Some of his *Colloquies* are satires on religious practices that Erasmus thought stupid or superstitious, yet he honors the formal requirements of the genre. In "The Funeral," for instance, the speakers describe two starkly contrasting models of dying "like a true Christian"—the first characterized by anxiety and an overload of religious paraphernalia, the second by a simple confidence in God's mercy. The dialogue ends with one of the speakers saying: "Each of these men was my friend. Perhaps I am not a fair judge of which died in a manner more becoming a Christian."[25]

The revival of these genres, immensely important for the development of Western literature, helped ground the humanist movement. By far the most significant grounding, however, was an institution, the humanistic school, whose origins date from the early fifteenth century. For their educational program the humanists took a step that their counterparts in the universities never did: they composed treatises and wrote letters that described their project, clarified its rationale, and acted as propaganda for it. In this endeavor they had models from antiquity from which to draw—various works of Cicero like the *Orator* and *De oratore,* after 1411 the Latin translation of the work on education ascribed to Plutarch, and especially Quintilian's now fully recovered *Institutiones.* The humanists from Pier Paolo Vergerio at the very beginning of the fifteenth century until Erasmus in the sixteenth thus made their case with Europe's elite. Theirs has to be one of the most successful advertising campaigns in history. The humanists not only established an institution; they supported it with an ongoing public-relations campaign.

Vergerio, a product of culture two in that he had pursued an Arts degree at the University of Bologna and later degrees in medicine and law at Padua, became one of the most influential promoters of two aspects of the *studia humanitatis.* He was the first humanist to adapt classical rhetoric to Christian preaching, displayed especially in a series of panegyrics on St. Jerome that he delivered in Padua. It was a spark that caught and that would, by the middle of the sixteenth century, transform preaching for both Catholics and Protestants alike. Its impact would continue to be felt well into the twentieth century.

Vergerio's use of principles of rhetoric resulted in holy speeches that were different from both the homily and the Scholastic sermon. The study of classical rhetoric as essential to the composition and delivery of "sacred orations" won an important and secure place in seminaries of almost every Christian church. Its ecclesiastical status promoted the already widespread persuasion that any speech of worth, sacred or secular, needed to be based on classical rhetoric.

Second, Vergerio composed, probably in 1403, *De ingenuis moribus et liberalibus studiis,* the first of the humanists' treatises on education. It was copied and recopied in manuscript, and it eventually ran through many printed editions. It was radically student-centered. It began with general principles of pedagogy, almost pedagogical psychology, expounding how the teacher must adapt to the temperament and situation of the student. This segued not to presentation of a curriculum but to reflection on how a boy's character needs to be molded to produce an honest and socially concerned adult, the aim of "liberal studies." He says, "We call those studies liberal, then, which are worthy of a free man; they are those through which virtue and wisdom are either practiced or sought, and by which the body or mind is disposed towards all the best things."[26]

Addressed to Ubertino, son of Francesco Carrara, the lord of Padua, the treatise implies throughout that the education it describes is intended for persons with a future career in public service, including the military. For that purpose the program must accomplish its task as quickly as possible and not be protracted into a lifetime of study or speculation—or, as we would say, into a lifetime of research: "One should not over-indulge in the liberal arts or linger over them in pursuit of perfection. For someone who dedicates himself completely to theory and the delights of literature perchance becomes dear to himself, but whether a prince or a private citizen, he is surely of little use to the city."[27] Implicit is the understanding that the program would be completed while the student was still in his teens. Implicit also is the understanding that the program is sufficient in itself and not, as such, a preparation for further studies in the university.

The three core disciplines in Vergerio's program are history, moral philosophy, and rhetoric. Each has its own merits, but an ethical concern connects them. History is in effect moral philosophy and practical prudence teaching by examples, both good and bad. Moral philosophy, the branch of philosophy most pertinent to the human situation, lays down precepts. Rhetoric leads to the communication of policies and the making of decisions advantageous to the common good. Vergerio fits other disciplines from the trivium and quadrivium into this scheme without entering into particulars. Dialectic/logic is subordinate to rhetoric. Unlike many other humanist educators, Vergerio makes ample room for science, namely, natural philosophy.

The next humanist to write for the cause was Leonardo Bruni, whose short treatise is particularly revealing because it is addressed to a woman, Battista Malatesta of Montefeltro. Beginning in antiquity with Sappho, women found a place and even a voice in this culture that they would not find in culture two until very recently, and this tradition was honored in the Renaissance. Boccaccio's series of biographical portraits of famous women, *De claris mulieribus,* sounds very contemporary in its criticism of historians who leave women out of their narratives.

The humanists' treatises projected an attractive vision. But something more practical was needed, and it was provided by Vittorino da Feltre. He was a student of a student of Petrarch and beginning in 1422 holder of the chair of rhetoric at the University of Padua. Deeply religious, he was convinced that education missed the point if it did not aim at influencing the character of the students, and he was distressed that the university made no provisions along these lines for the younger students, in their early or mid-teens. On a private level Vittorino had for years been offering lessons in various subjects in which he practiced and experimented with techniques and principles that would make effective the general ideals animating the humanist movement. In 1423 he resigned his position at Padua to open his own school in Venice. Just as he got started, he received an invitation from Gianfrancesco Gonzaga, marquis of Mantua, to establish a school for his children and the children of leading citizens in the area.

Vittorino remained at Mantua until his death more than twenty years later. In the course of those years he taught boys and a few girls ranging in age from four to twenty. Most were from highborn families, but he took in a few others when convinced of their talent and probity. He trained a number of students who would later assume important public roles, like Federico da Montefeltro, the future duke of Urbino. What we know about Vittorino and his school we know from the recollections of his former students, who were unanimous in their admiration and even affection for him.

Vittorino's curriculum centered on the great works of Latin literature—Cicero and Virgil of course, but ranging beyond them even to Augustine. For the best students he provided instruction in Greek, so that they might read Demosthenes, Sophocles, Xenophon, and other Greek authors up to John Chrysostom. The academic curriculum was only part of a larger vision of education, which Vittorino conducted in a house set apart from the court called the Casa Giocosa, "the Pleasant House," whose very name indicates the learning atmosphere he tried to create. Moreover, as the classical treatises prescribed, he made physical exercise part of the daily routine.

At one point the student population rose to about seventy. For dealing with such a large number Vittorino imported scholars to help him, especially for instruction in Greek, and he also engaged older students to deal, under his supervision, with younger ones. In accord with what the treatises inculcated, he believed that the most important teaching was conveyed by the person of the teacher. In that teaching he, by his gentleness, the care he displayed for each student, and his obvious integrity and religious devotion, seems to have been uncommonly successful.

Vittorino was a rare genius. His school disappeared with him. Italian cities and families provided a "primary and secondary" education for their sons that by the middle of the fifteenth century was largely based on classical authors, though it seems to have been generally untouched by the high-sounding goals the humanists proposed. Not until the next century would the system mature on a widespread basis in both Italy and the rest of Europe, and not until the seventeenth century would it reach its apogee. The schools won easy acceptance, it seems, wherever they were introduced. They promised much. Sending one's sons to them became the vogue.

The pedagogues the system displaced or replaced had no organized voice to protest and seem just to have faded away or gradually accommodated, probably on a minimal basis, to the changes in their profession. The university professors in the Arts faculty, on the contrary, made noise, and wars erupted over the nature of "true philosophy" and its method. The professors in the theological faculties felt even more on the defensive.

The assault on theology teachers was evident early on. In his treatise on education, Bruni cautioned Battista Malatesta against them: "By learning I do not mean that confused and vulgar sort such as is possessed by those who nowadays profess theology."[28] Lorenzo Valla, in a panegyric in 1455 supposedly honoring Thomas Aquinas, compared him unfavorably to the Fathers of the Church. But it was Erasmus who emerged in the first decades of the sixteenth century as the great champion of the style of the Fathers in opposition to that of the academic theologians.

Erasmus sometimes delighted in venom, as we saw in his letter to Thomas Grey. His most widely circulated work was *Praise of Folly,* in which he took out in serious jest against every way of life and profession, including the humanists. He reserved his most incisive criticism, however, for the academic theologians. With all the other professions Folly's message was that they were doing a good thing but badly. With the theologians Folly's message, on the contrary, was that they were doing a bad thing all too well.

The section dealing with theologians is long, repeating in different words the same criticisms, most of which pertain to style of discourse. Folly sums up these criticisms when she reprimands the theologians for "speaking with a profane tongue" and arguing "with the pagan subtlety of the heathen," thereby polluting "the majesty of divine theology with words and sentiments that are so trivial and even squalid. Yet those who do so are so happy in their self-satisfaction and self-congratulation, and so busy night and day with these enjoyable tomfooleries, that they haven't even a spare moment in which to read the Gospel or the letters of Paul even once through."[29]

The Scholastics did not really know the Bible. What Erasmus meant was that, though they quoted it constantly, they knew it as a quarry from which to draw arguments and not as a collection of literary and historical texts in which meaning was inseparable from context and genre. To know the Bible was to know it in its original languages and at the same time to interpret each of its books according to the appropriate genres and the intent of the authors.

In 1516 Erasmus published the first critical edition of the Greek New Testament, along with a new Latin translation. Petrarch's summons "back to the sources" had helped launch humanists' search for good manuscripts from which to construct reliable versions of their texts, leading them ever deeper into the historical situations and literary forms that constituted them. By the mid-fifteenth century Valla had turned that concern to the Greek New Testament, the text supreme, and he was able to show inaccuracies and misunderstandings in the Latin Vulgate edition, the one in almost universal use in the Western church. Moreover, by using arguments from internal evidence—word usage, historical inconsistencies, and so forth—he was able to show that the "Donation of Constantine," a document purportedly written by the emperor in the early fourth century granting the pope governance of Rome and even more, was a forgery from a later time. The art of textual and historical criticism was coming into being. Erasmus' New Testament was the almost inevitable outcome. At the same time he began publishing critical editions of the Latin and Greek Fathers, beginning with St. Jerome, his favorite among the Latins, and including eventually Origen, his favorite among the Greeks.

For Erasmus these editions of the New Testament and the Fathers were not exercises without pastoral import. He felt he could criticize Scholastic theology because he had an alternative to offer: a return to the more literary and rhetorical style of the Fathers. That was the "ancient and genuine" theology, quite different from the "modern" theology. It was genuine because it was drawn directly from the sacred texts and because it led to a "theological life." It touched the heart and centered on the few truths that were essential to Christianity rather than on the secondary issues the Scholastics pursued.

The ultimate basis for theology was the Bible, now viewed as a collection of texts composed over a long period of time by a variety of authors using different genres. It would yield its meaning and teachings only if these factors were taken into account. But there was an even more sublime dimension, especially to the gospels. In his introduction to the first edition of his Greek New Testament, Erasmus advocated translating the Bible into the vernacular and placing it in the hands of all who could read. His concluding words are almost rhapsodic. In the New Testament Christians find not only inspiration but Christ himself, truly present: "These writings bring you the living image of his holy mind and the speaking, healing, dying, rising Christ himself, and thus they render him so fully present that you would see less if you gazed upon him with your very eyes."[30]

These are powerful words. Erasmus has nothing so strong to say about works from the corpus of classical literature, the core of the humanist curriculum. He assumes they are to be read as models of eloquence. Yet he further sees that literature as stirring the heart to virtue and therefore being more valuable to the soul than the writings of Scholastic theologians. In "The Godly Feast," the most sublime of his *Colloquies,* he has one of the interlocutors say that

> whatever is devout and contributes to good morals should not be called profane. Sacred Scripture is of course the basic authority in everything, yet I sometimes run across ancient sayings or pagan writings—even the poets—so purely and reverently and admirably expressed that I can't help believing their authors' hearts were moved by some divine power. And perhaps the spirit of Christ is more widespread than we understand, and the company of saints includes many not in our calendar. Speaking frankly among friends, I can't read Cicero's *De senectute, De amicitia, De officiis, De Tusculanis quaestionibus* without sometimes kissing the book and blessing that pure heart, divinely inspired as it was . . . I would much rather let all of Scotus and others of that sort perish than the books of a single Cicero or Plutarch.[31]

Erasmus, drawing on sources ancient and contemporary, had formulated a "new" theological vision, and he did so in self-conscious opposition to the theological establishment. In that regard there was a touch of the prophet in him. By his own definition the Scholastics were an arrogant, cantankerous, and ignorant lot, so he should not have been surprised at the vehemence and bitterness with which they returned his volleys and with which they would pursue him to the end of his days—and even beyond. They were shocked that he would tamper with the Latin text of the Bible, which had been in use for so many centuries. In his commentaries and other works they found heresy. And, even more fundamental, they dismissed him as a mere grammarian. It was not their method but his that was awry, radically flawed. Never before or since have cultures two and three more patently bared the incompatible parts within them, and never before or since (not even today!) have they been more viciously at each other's throats.

It was a Scholastic theologian who coined the label that stuck: Erasmus laid the egg that Luther hatched. As the religious controversies heated up, that label or its equivalent rallied against him not only much of the academic establishment but also Catholic churchmen and even politicians. By the time Erasmus died in 1536, still revered in many circles and widely read, he had become a scandal for partisans on both sides of the religious divide. After the outbreak of the Reformation he expressed regret that he had been so caustic in some of his criticisms. True to the traditions of culture three, he urged moderation on both sides and urged conversation and compromise. These were not viable options for Protestant prophets, who found him soft, a chameleon, untrustworthy. Catholic polemicists assessed him the same way; he had in 1525 separated himself from Luther but not far enough for their taste—deep down he must still be in Luther's camp. In 1559 the Spanish and Roman Inquisitions proscribed all his writings, even the grammatical works, thereby making them forbidden books.

Beyond the Renaissance

Petrarch, Valla, and Erasmus perceived incompatibilities between cultures two and three. They had sighted the enemy and wanted to bring him down. Others missed or dismissed the incompatibilities. Just as from the beginning of the humanist movement many clerics in Italy who had been trained in culture two also pursued "good letters" enthusiastically, many laymen trained in the faculties of law and medicine would later do the same. In the seventeenth century this impulse toward reconciliation for the most part prevailed. It was the age of science. It was the age of eloquence.

In the seventeenth century culture three seemed reconciled within itself in particularly harmonious fashion, as both its poetic and rhetorical impulses sometimes notably bore fruit in the same person. Milton, of course, provides a clear example of somebody who combined poetic contemplation with an active role in the great events of his day. He wrote "L'Allegro" and "Il Penseroso" probably while in his early twenties and first published "Paradise Lost" thirty years later. Meanwhile, besides writing other important poetry, he waded into public controversy with pamphlets on, for example, reform of the church and the rightness of divorce on grounds of incompatibility. He served in Oliver Cromwell's government as Latin secretary for foreign affairs.

Thus humanists could afford to be generous, for their success seemed palpable: "good letters" and eloquence needed no defense by the seventeenth century. They had, moreover, succeeded in convincing European leaders that the only sound program for "primary and secondary" education was the program they proposed. They somehow did not have to answer very seriously for the weaknesses in the program, such as its vagueness about how literature inspires to goodness and the strangeness of acquiring eloquence in languages that nobody spoke in ordinary dealings. Theirs was a success story. The humanists helped create the demand for a certain type of schooling, and they then supplied the product. True, other forms of formal instruction burgeoned at this time, such as vernacular schools for boys from lower socioeconomic status and a more widespread and publicly organized catechesis, where reading was often taught. But the humanistic school had won an astounding pan-European acceptance.

As happened with the universities, the institutional grounding of culture three as an educational enterprise resulted in the creation of symbols and rites, sometimes in half-aware imitation of the universities. Perhaps the most striking symbol to emerge was the school building itself. In the fifteenth century humanist "schools" in Italy were usually one-teacher enterprises often conducted in a private home. By the end of the sixteenth century the Jesuits, for instance, were building elaborate complexes, with multiple courtyards, residences for both faculty and students, large classrooms, and sometimes a theater. Faculties now began to comprise eight to ten or many more teachers. Prizes were awarded, and the ritual of lectures and examinations was firmly in place. Later came school colors, banners, sometimes uniforms, sports teams, and networks of "old boys" and then of "old girls."

For the Christian churches the impact of the humanistic philosophy of education was immense. The humanists argued that the study of pagan works promoted the formation of good character that resulted in a responsible and effective Christian adult. In England in the eighteenth and nineteenth centuries, training for Holy Orders was substantially training in classical literature. Athens had much to do with Jerusalem. It was the humanistic rationale that prompted both Catholic and Protestant churchmen to throw their support behind the program, which in many cases led to the actual sponsoring, staffing, and managing of schools, a new phenomenon in the history of the West. The Jesuits are the single most obvious case in a development that we take almost for granted.

By the seventeenth century the Jesuits were running hundreds of schools in Europe and overseas. They took as an article of faith that the *studia humanitatis* were ordered to the common good and the betterment of society. In 1551, just as the order was beginning to undertake such schools, Juan Alfonso Polanco, the secretary of the order, summarized for its members the results to be hoped for: "Those who are today only students will grow up to be pastors, civic officials, administrators of justice, and will fill other important posts to everybody's profit and advantage."[32] Although they were confessional schools in a confessional age, the Jesuit schools had a civic purpose that transcended the confessional differences. The same could be said of the correlative Protestant schools, and of course of schools run by municipalities and other entities. The Jesuits also took it as an article of faith that pagan literature was a source for ethical and religious inspiration. As Cornelius a Lapide, an important Jesuit exegete, said about a passage from Epictetus, "O wonder, these words ring of the Gospel, not just moral philosophy."[33]

The program the humanist theorists envisaged went beyond texts and classroom, however, to include other skills like fencing and horsemanship required by the students' social status, and it was generally concerned with their physical development and well-being. By the seventeenth century the Jesuits had developed an extensive array of "extra-curriculars" in their schools. Like other educators in the tradition, they had come to believe that the character formation at the heart of the enterprise was fostered as much by these activities as by anything that took place in the classroom—fostered, that is, by sports, school dramas, membership in religious confraternities, and participation in a wide variety of school-related festivities.

In the seventeenth century the Christian began to acquire a somewhat new profile, a profile articulated and promulgated on a basis that transcended national and even confessional backgrounds. He was refined in speech and manners. His style was courteous, and he acted in accord with principle—innocent, it seems, of Machiavelli. The aristocracy inherited long-standing traditions of courtly culture. The source of the profile does not lie, therefore, exclusively in the cultivation of the *studia*. Through the *studia*, however, the traditions become newly styled. *Urbanità, politezza, cortesia, conversazione,* and *civiltà* are the words that emerge to express the ideal. Graceful and urbane interaction in pleasant social circumstances had early on been dramatized effectively in Castiglione's *Book of the Courtier* and made attractive. Because in urban centers the schools attracted boys from modest backgrounds, the ideals were communicated beyond the cream of the elite.

The ideal underwent modifications in different countries over the course of time. The English "gentleman" was a clearly formulated type by the nineteenth century. He was unfailingly courteous and espoused "fair play" and "conduct befitting a gentleman" in all undertakings. He was modest in demeanor and self-effacing about accomplishments. Nothing was socially more unacceptable than appearing slick. Newman in his *Idea of a University* has a long and well-known description of such a gentleman, who, for instance: "makes light of favors while he does them and seems to be receiving when he is conferring. . . . He is never mean or little in his disputes, never takes unfair advantage, never mistakes personalities or sharp sayings for arguments, or insinuates evil which he dare not say out. . . . He has too much good sense to be affronted at insults, he is too well employed to remember injuries, and too indolent to bear malice."[34]

This is the gentleman that Reginald Johnston held up as an ideal to Pu Yi. This gentleman, as Newman describes him, could not be further from the denunciatory prophet of culture one, for "the true gentleman . . . carefully avoids whatever may cause a jar or a jolt in the minds of those with whom he is cast—all clashing of opinion, or collision of feeling, all restraint, or suspicion, or gloom, or resentment; his great concern is to make every one at their ease and at home." The gentleman is far from culture one, but he would also have a difficult time in faculty meetings of culture two.

So much for the gentleman, but what about the gentle lady? Vittorino had included girls in his Casa Giocosa, and other educators offered instruction to women. Examples of humanistically schooled women abound, from Thomas More's daughter Meg to Queen Elizabeth herself. But the schools, as they developed in the sixteenth century, were for boys. In seventeenth-century France that situation began to change significantly. The Jesuits at Bordeaux, for instance, persuaded the baroness Jeanne de Lestonnac to organize a group of women to establish schools for girls that generally corresponded to the Jesuits' schools for boys. Thus in 1606 was founded the Filles de Notre Dame, the first female teaching order to receive official church approval in France. Others followed. The Ursulines, however, became the most esteemed and widespread such order of women in France—and in New France. By the eighteenth century in France alone the Ursulines had more than ten thousand members distributed over three hundred communities. These communities were charged with providing free instruction and education to young girls.

The convent school emerged as a characteristic institution of French culture in the *ancien régime.* Devastated by the Revolution, it revived in the nineteenth century and soon became a mark of Catholic society everywhere. The Baroness de Lestonnac promised a modest program of reading, writing, and needlework, that is, "all the accomplishments suitable for well-brought-up young women."[35] The more ambitious curriculum of the *studia humanitatis,* adapted to what were considered female roles, soon made inroads, however, and in some schools it was comparable to the curriculum offered to men.

Typical of the program of "young ladies' academies" in the early twentieth century was the curriculum followed by all the students at Mount de Chantal Academy in remote Wheeling, West Virginia: four years of Latin, six years of either French or German language and literature, ancient and modern history, some six or seven plays of Shakespeare, and assorted English and American poetry and novels. To this were added, among other subjects, courses in botany, chemistry, astronomy, geometry, trigonometry—and logic and rhetoric. Pupils were admitted at age twelve and remained for six or seven years, for a total student population of about one hundred.

Protestantism did not have Catholicism's network of female religious orders to carry out such programs, but through schools of various kinds, most of them of religious inspiration or affiliation, the same process took place, with the same ideals, the same faith in them, and almost identical curriculum. The aim for both Catholic and Protestant (or neither) was the same, a woman of refined tastes. Within the framework of the social status quo, the aim was also a woman with a sense of responsibility to society at large. Eleanor Roosevelt said of Allenswood, the school outside London where she was a pupil and which she remembered with great affection, that whatever she had become since then had its seeds in those years.

Ideals like these from culture three were communicated outside the schools. The reconciliation between cultures two and three was matched by a close affiliation between three and four. The revival of the *studia* entailed performance. If the education was to leave its impress upon students, orations had to be delivered, not just studied; poetry had to be recited, not just read; plays had to be staged. The plays were usually open to the public, and they represented on a minor scale the general enthusiasm of the age for the theater. It is estimated that in Shakespeare's England people attended plays as often as people today attend movies.

With plays came music and dance. Then came the other arts. At Mount de Chantal, "all branches of music are taught on the plan of the best classical conservatories," with "Soirées Musicales" held in the Music Room every month. The department of art was "conducted on the plan of the best art schools in the country," with instruction in drawing, illustration, design, and painting in oil and watercolor. There were no courses in needlework or any of the practical arts of homemaking.[36]

In the United States by the early twentieth century elements of the humanistic curriculum were offered to both boys and girls in the public schools operated by municipalities. Teenagers who followed that curriculum knew by heart, in Latin, the opening words of Julius Caesar's *Gallic Wars,* "All Gaul is divided into three parts." Knowledge of Latin was a requisite for entering many universities. Schools knew that what they were about was, somehow, "for God and country."

In the early decades of the twentieth century culture three in its Renaissance form seemed relatively secure in the United States, but challenges to it, long in the making, began to surface and have impact. The great humanists of the Italian Renaissance extolled the literary excellence of the classics of ancient Greece and Rome, but this does not mean they were unappreciative of vernacular literature or disdainful of it. No Italian wanted to minimize what Dante had achieved with the *Commedia.* Petrarch was proud of his *Canzoniere.* Boccaccio wrote effectively in Latin on subjects of concern to humanists, but his masterpiece, immediately recognized as such, was the *Decameron.* In the early sixteenth century, Pietro Bembo was the great arbiter of literary taste in Italy for both Latin and vernacular literature. The great vernacular authors from the fifteenth century forward had, moreover, a broader view of literature than the didacticism that was never far from somebody like Erasmus.

Nonetheless, from the beginning of the humanist movement the program in the schools did not reflect this appreciation for the vernacular or make room for it. As mentioned, at Cambridge in the early seventeenth century the curriculum over a four-year course was heavily biased in favor of the literary texts from Roman and Greek antiquity, and it included, as would be true for most schools outside the influence of the Catholic inquisitions, the *Colloquies* of Erasmus. But it contained not a single work in English. In that regard Cambridge was unexceptional.

The very success of installing literature so prominently in the curriculum helped in the long run to subvert the preeminence of the classical texts. In Rome as early as 1610, for instance, Jesuits at the Roman College were translating plays into the vernacular for performance. By the second half of the century French had replaced Latin as the international language of diplomacy and of intellectual and literary communication. If in culture two faith in the sacrosanct status of Greek science had been successfully challenged, and if in culture four Michelangelo was held to have surpassed all previous achievement, the retrospective bias of the *studia humanitatis* could not go unchallenged for long.

In some circles in the seventeenth century the belief was that the ancient writers were superior to modern works in the vernacular, and the curriculum supported this persuasion. At that very time, however, the brilliance of "the moderns" was ever more evident and taken for granted, and it was exploding in unmistakable manifestations of genius—Tasso, Cervantes, Lope de Vega, Montaigne, Corneille, Molière, Shakespeare, Sidney, Milton. To say nothing of the older authors like Dante, Petrarch, and Boccaccio. The discrepancy, not surprisingly, gave rise to debate.

This was the origin of the "Quarrel of the Ancients and the Moderns," which, long simmering, erupted in the latter part of the century. Two French works—Charles Perrault's *Parallel of the Ancients and Moderns* (1688–1696) and Bernard Fontenelle's *Digression on the Ancients and Moderns* (1688)—set off the most focused phase of the controversy. In the course of it the superiority of the one over the other was adamantly defended, but at this point no one argued for the elimination of the ancients from the curriculum.

A result of the quarrel was, nonetheless, a gradual broadening of the literary program of the "Latin Schools." While Latin remained a staple in the program, its piece of the curricular pie became ever smaller as vernacular works cut out for themselves more and more of it. At Mount de Chantal in the early twentieth century, as we saw, students studied Latin for four years but, besides works in English, devoted five or six to either French or German. The development was analogous to what happened in antiquity when the Romans gradually replaced Greek works in the curriculum with their own Latin masterpieces. On the Continent similar changes in the curriculum reflect the growing nationalism that in the nineteenth century exalted native cultural products over foreign.

By that century, in any case, it was becoming ever more difficult to defend even the more restricted place of "the classics" in the curriculum. They had their spirited advocates, often churchmen, like Edward Copleston, provost of Oriel, later a bishop and dean of St. Paul's. Oxford deemed his defense in 1810 so meritorious that it granted him in view of it the degree of Doctor of Divinity. Study of the classics, Copleston argued, resulted in "a cultivation of the mind." This was a recent and curiously vague argument that, though often repeated, probably added to the skepticism about the classics rather than dispelled it. It continued to be repeated into the twentieth century. The cause was not helped by the stodgy "classicist" mentality with which some of its promoters seemed imbued—the persuasion that the best thoughts had long ago been thought, the best phrases turned, the best books written.

In secondary schools, moreover, especially as time devoted to the classics diminished, students rarely progressed far enough in their grasp of Greek and Latin syntax to appreciate the literary quality of the texts. Their teachers were often not able to make credible connections between the text and the ideals of civility and service, nor were they even aware that they were expected to do so.

Rhetoric, especially in its primary sense of oratory, came under attack, once again, in the nineteenth century, more viciously on the Continent than in England or North America. After the American Civil War, Harvard College built Memorial Hall as a tribute to its sons from the Union side who had fallen in combat. The hall, which from the outside looks like a neo-gothic church, is more precisely a temple to rhetoric, for running around the outside wall is a series of niches with busts of great orators like Demosthenes, Chrysostom, Cicero, Bossuet, Burke, and Daniel Webster. Rhetoric still held its head high.

Yet at about the same time Ernest Renan delivered a powerful and influential address to the Académie française in which he denounced rhetoric as "the only error of the Greeks." He held the Jesuits principally responsible for foisting this aberration onto the public through their schools, another instance of the obscurantism for which the order was well known. Rhetoric was a discipline of the *ancien régime.* Renan's message fell on willing ears. Within the decade the French government suppressed the teaching of rhetoric in public *lycées.* If not banned in other parts of Europe or in North America, rhetoric began in those places to seem at best old-fashioned.

In their treatises on the subject, the Renaissance humanists produced a fully articulated philosophy of education. At the time they had no rivals in such articulation, but by the twentieth century a number of other full-blown philosophies were in circulation, some of which denied the assumption that there was one curriculum suitable for all, another assault on the Renaissance ideal. In the United States after World War II the influx of large numbers of immigrants from non-Western societies further compromised the status not only of the "ancients" but also of the "moderns" of the West.

Developments like these are well known and have been endlessly discussed. Another, less-noticed but equally significant development has had important implications for culture three in secondary schools, the venues in which the culture has found its most secure institutional base since the Renaissance: For students with sufficient intelligence and ambition, these schools are no longer deemed sufficient in themselves but considered largely preparation for university. The "Latin Schools" have become "Prep Schools." They prepare students for culture two. The teachers in the prep schools have themselves been trained in the Graduate School of culture two, the helpmate but also the hungry rival of culture three.

In North America the primary and secondary schools run by the churches have in different ways always maintained that they had a purpose beyond a successful here-and-now. Besides their specifically academic and religious goals for their students, some of them espouse a social goal that is at least reminiscent of the concern for the common good that has been a constitutive element of the rhetorical aspect of culture three from the beginning. The Jesuits, for instance, sponsor more than fifty "prep" schools in the United States, and they profess in their literature that one of their goals is inspiring their students to be "men and women for others." In effect if not in intent that expression is a paraphrase of Cicero's statement, "We are not born for ourselves alone," quoted earlier in the chapter.

But culture three is not essentially an educational program or a specific literary theory. It is incomparably larger. Its real home is in the larger world. Culture three is Homer, who never went to school, and then Sophocles, Virgil, Bernard, Dante, Shakespeare, Molière, Eliot and Austen, Wilde and Joyce, Faulkner and Hemingway, as well as their successors up to the present.

We no longer subscribe to the didacticism that undergirded much of the literary theory of the past. We read these authors because they give aesthetic pleasure. They give it, however, largely through authentic depiction of characters and situations, which are mirrors of the complexities and ambiguities of our own experience. They deal with ambition and fear. They deal with greed and redemption. They deal with love and hate, and they deal with the problem of sometimes not knowing the difference. They weave webs with words that reflect the webs we weave with our lives. The webs we weave are not neat geometrical patterns; they contain tangles and knots. We read these authors because we somehow find in them help in negotiating our way through such webs.

In the mid-twentieth century culture three had a moment of brilliance in the religious sphere. That was the Second Vatican Council, which met in Saint Peter's basilica for four long periods over the course of four years, from 1962 until 1965, with the participation of some 2,500 bishops and perhaps even more theologians. It has been described as the most important religious event of the twentieth century, and it brings us back to the question of style.

Erasmus and others in the sixteenth century campaigned to change the style of theological discourse. They had limited success at best, much of which was blunted beginning in the nineteenth century with the spread to seminaries and divinity schools of the *Wissenschaft* ideal, which in quite different ways affected both Protestant and Catholic theological style. The Catholic situation was unique among the churches because for the first time the papacy began prescribing the content of the curriculum for seminaries and similar institutions. In 1879 Pope Leo XIII in his encyclical "Aeterni patris" made normative the philosophy/theology of Thomas Aquinas, which necessarily included the concomitant Aristotelian substructure.

This neo-Scholastic phenomenon had a prophetic aspect, for almost universally until the 1930s the revived Thomism was conceived as an antidote to all modern philosophers beginning with Descartes and was used as a club with which to beat them. Not surprisingly, this had the result of isolating the Catholic intellectual enterprise from the intellectual mainstream except by way of polemic. The polemical aspect further sharpened the intellectually aggressive character of medieval academic discourse. This meant that the neo-Thomism of the late nineteenth and early twentieth centuries, before it was moderated by scholars like Jacques Maritain and Étienne Gilson, conformed in its own peculiar way to the aggressive character of the "scientific" discourse surging into the universities at the same time—indeed, it even went beyond it. Take no hostages. Especially in seminary textbooks, obligatory in all seminaries, which were the only places theology was taught, neo-Thomism conformed to that aggressive character in that it approached all issues in an unremittingly intellectualized way but went beyond it with apodictic proofs based on self-evident truths demonstrated with irrefutable logic. It was a caricature of culture two.

This context makes the culture-three style of discourse that characterizes the documents of Vatican Council II all the more remarkable. That style did not, of course, spring out of nowhere. In Germany and Belgium but especially in France, theologians had for several decades been trying to find alternatives to the rigidity of the dominant style, and a number of them turned to the Fathers in what they called a *resourcement,* a "return to the sources." As it turns out, the documents of the council often read like a commentary or homily by one of the Fathers—or by Erasmus. A greater contrast with the style of discourse of the Council of Trent would be difficult to find. Vatican II, like Luther, was a "language-event."

Before the council opened, there was much speculation about what doctrine it might "define." Defining, from the language-game of culture two, as in Trent, is what councils did. The council in fact defined nothing. On some basic level the participants in the council realized that definition, indispensable though it sometimes is, sets one apart from others, hardens lines of division, and makes reconciliation more difficult. Why not, instead, seek as far as possible common ground with other believers and even with nonbelievers? To accomplish such a goal, a rhetorical, not a dialectical, style was required. Perhaps the single most operative word in the council, which occurs again and again in the documents, is *dialogue,* a word germane to culture three.

The implication is that in dialogue each side listens to the other, and as a result each will modify its stance a little. Dialogue or colloquy does not define a subject but opens conversation on it. One of the important goals of the council, as it evolved, was trust and cooperation among the Christian churches, which had been at one another's throats since the Reformation. In accord with the ethos of culture three, those churches were now invited to sit down at a holy negotiating table.

The documents published by the council manifest many of the characteristics of epideictic rhetoric, for they want to raise appreciation for the issues at stake and to celebrate them. They abound in metaphor and analogies, and they engage for the most part in a discourse of congratulation. Often the intent is to bring people together around some shared value and to encourage horizontal relationships and a sense of *collegiality,* another of the council's most characteristic words.

The council illustrates two realities at the heart of this book. First, it provides a sustained example of how form influences content. How the Christian teachings were proposed in the council influenced which ones were presented and the mode they assumed. Bishops, for instance, were presented not as enforcers of discipline, as they were at Trent, but as coordinators of the efforts of all those engaged with them in a common cause. Second, it provides a striking example of how difficult it can be for the cultures to understand one another. To this day the council has become an object of confusion and controversy, to a large extent because interpreters miss that they are dealing here with literary genres altogether different from those of all preceding councils. This obliviousness is all the more amazing because the first thing that strikes one when reading the documents is that they are written in a style no previous council ever adopted.

What has Athens to do with Jerusalem? The popes of the nineteenth and early twentieth centuries assumed a severely prophetic stance toward Athens in almost all its modern forms. The council never explicitly repudiated that stance, but almost from the beginning, encouraged by Pope John XXIII, it distanced itself from it. It did so, however, in the measured and reconciling style in which culture three is especially adept. That style is especially operative in the final and perhaps most telling document of the council, "The Church in the Modern World." The document is unprecedented for a council in being addressed not just to church members but to all men and women of good will.

The body of the text, while it takes account of the dark side of modern civilization, tries at the same time to raise appreciation for the positive. In some of the first pages it almost sings in praise of an old theme from culture three, the dignity of the human person, and then goes on to exhort to that other familiar theme, the need to work together for the common good—specifically to work together on issues such as poverty, war and peace, and the arms race.

The opening words of the document speak unmistakably with the vocabulary of culture three: "The joys and hopes and the sorrows and anxieties, especially of those who are poor and afflicted, are also the joys and hopes, sorrows and anxieties of the disciples of Christ, and there is nothing truly human that does not also affect them." No council, certainly not Trent, ever spoke like this about joys and sorrows. And in the expression "nothing truly human that does not also affect them" the allusion is clear. It is a paraphrase of one of the most famous lines in Latin literature, from the playwright Terence, "I am a man and therefore indifferent to nothing that is human."[37] That statement is the ultimate answer of culture three to the Athens/Jerusalem question.

CULTURE FOUR

Art and Performance

According to the story often told in 1988, when Soviet Russia decided to celebrate the millennium of Russia's conversion to Christianity, in 988 Prince Vladimir of Kiev sent out emissaries to discover the true religion. When the emissaries reached Constantinople and witnessed a liturgy there in Hagia Sophia, they knew they had achieved their goal. They returned to Kiev and reported to Vladimir: "We knew not whether we were in heaven or on earth, for surely there is no such splendor or beauty anywhere upon earth. We cannot describe it to you. Only this we know, that God dwells there among men, and that their service surpasses the worship of all other places. For we cannot forget its beauty."[1]

For all the importance of the three verbal cultures already dealt with, by far the most conspicuous is the material culture of Christianity. We may be innocent of prophets like Gregory VII, or academicians like Aquinas, or humanists like Erasmus, but every day of our lives we see churches on the streets of our cities. We see even more impressive ones in Europe, a few of which date back to the early Christian era and contain mosaics of extraordinary beauty. Museums are filled with paintings in fresco and oil with Christian themes, most of which originally graced churches, chapels, baptistries, sacristies, and private oratories especially from the twelfth through the seventeenth century.

The material culture of Christianity is overwhelming in its quantity, quality, and variety. As with the other three cultures, its story is inseparable from the Athens/Jerusalem issue and is a startling instance of massive appropriation, in its beginnings, of the cultural reality of the Greco-Roman world. This was apparent from the middle of the third century, but it burst into spectacular visibility almost immediately after the recognition of Christianity by Constantine in 313.

Presenting this culture is difficult because it entails talking about a reality that itself does not talk, except in some highly ritualized way. Culture four is essentially about physical beauty. While in its expression it is the most material of the four cultures, by eschewing words it is at the same time the most spiritual, even transcendent—"We knew not whether we were in heaven or on earth." Culture four is the culture of enchantment. It takes us from where we are to a place where human speech and human concepts fail: "We cannot describe it."

Vladimir's emissaries expressed the essential frustration of anyone resorting to words to deal with art, music, dance—with beauty. "If I could define it," Martha Graham purportedly replied when asked the meaning of a piece she had choreographed, "we would not have had to dance it." But this is a book, and it cannot be danced. It must use words.

The words that appear in the historical sources sometimes deserve quotation, but even when they express appreciation for culture four they invariably betray the verbal culture from which they originate, and they deal with it accordingly. Culture one values culture four as propaganda. Culture two sees it as ideas in disguise, and culture three as an incitement to devotion. But, though it may have such uses, it is none of these. Words that come a little closer to capturing the essence of the culture are *pleasure* and *play*.

Some sources especially from the early period express simple satisfaction in the beauty of the church or celebrate the celebration that is the performance. Even when they do, however, they remain extraneous to it, for they are speaking about what by definition is unspeakable.

Culture four produces beauty, and it can do so independent of the motivation of its patrons. Moreover, no matter what their conscious motivation in any given instance, Christians wanted beautiful objects and took satisfaction in beautiful performances. They saw these objects and performances not only as consonant with their religion but as integral to it. They hungered for the experience of beauty, and they took measures to make it happen.

Building and Outfitting the House of the Lord

Liturgy, broadly understood, is the fundamental context for Christian appropriation of the material culture of the Hellenistic world. The most impressive art and, without exception, architecture were produced in relationship to liturgy and as enhancement of it. A relatively large number of liturgical texts have come down to us containing the words that were said, but relatively few sources even from later periods describe in more than tantalizing asides the movement and ongoing action of the service. Despite this relative dearth, what is strikingly clear is that the performance of the liturgy after 313, when it moved into great public spaces, was transformed into a much more solemn, visually impressive, and public spectacle.

In that development Christians were inspired by descriptions of the magnificence of worship in the Old Testament. The Temple of Solomon glistened with an overlay of gold and gems and was furnished with an altar of bronze, ten golden lampstands, and a great array of vessels of pure gold. The priests wore costly and colorful garments. "Hymns and canticles" were sung. David danced before the Ark of the Covenant. Psalm after psalm enjoined "singing joyfully to the Lord." (This is a Jerusalem quite different from Tertullian's.) But as Christians in the fourth century tried in their imagination to reconstruct such splendor, they had immediately before their eyes not those chronologically and culturally distant realities but the material culture of the late Roman Empire.

Despite a few dissenting voices, Christian leaders in the fourth century had no scruples about the burgeoning magnificence of their liturgical edifices or about the elaborate furnishings and decorations that outfitted them. Indeed, they could hardly have been more enthusiastic. They insisted that the end result be a beauty and splendor almost beyond description. This is what the artists, artisans, and architects were striving for. This is what moved the soul of the beholder.

While surely not innocent of the didactic and propagandistic aspects of the objects of their praise, speakers consistently come back to their aesthetic excellence. Egeria, that observant pilgrim from the West in the late fourth century, described the church in Bethlehem: "The decorations are too marvelous for words. All you can see is gold and jewels and silk . . . everything they use is made of gold and jewels. You simply cannot imagine the number and the sheer weight of the candles and the tapers and lamps and everything they use for the services. They are beyond description, and so is the magnificent building itself."[2]

Procopius was no great lover of Justinian, the builder of Hagia Sophia, but his description of the church reveals the captivation with sheer physical beauty and the appreciation of it that characterized those involved:

> The church has become a spectacle of marvelous beauty, overwhelming to those who see it. . . . It exults in an indescribable beauty. For it proudly reveals its mass and the harmony of its proportions, having neither excess nor

> deficiency. . . . It abounds exceedingly in sunlight and in the reflection of the sun's rays from the marble. Indeed, one might say that its interior is not illuminated from without by the sun, but that the radiance comes into being within it, such an abundance of light bathes this shrine. . . . All these details produce a single and most extraordinary harmony in the work, and yet do not permit the spectator to linger much over the study of any one of them, but each detail attracts the eye and draws it on irresistibly to itself.
>
> And whenever anyone enters this church to pray, he understands at once that it is not by human power or skill but by the influence of God that this work has been so finely turned out. And so his mind is lifted up toward God and exalted, feeling that he cannot be far away, but must especially love to dwell in this place that he has chosen.[3]

Upon entering Hagia Sophia for the first time, Justinian supposedly exclaimed, "Solomon, I have triumphed over you!" If he did so triumph, it is no wonder, for he marshaled the resources of the empire to build a church he hoped would surpass all others. In so doing he followed in the pattern set by the first great Christian builder, his predecessor Constantine. Constantine's letter to Bishop Macarius of Jerusalem, reported by Eusebius, is famous for indicating the imperial prodigality in the erection of his great basilicas in Rome, Constantinople, and Palestine:

> It befits your Sagacity to make such arrangements and such provision of every necessary thing, that not only shall this basilica be the finest in the world but that everything else, too, shall be of such quality that all the most beautiful buildings of every city may be surpassed by this one. As regards the construction and decoration of the walls, know that we have entrusted that to the care of our friend Dracilianus . . . and to

> the governor of the province [who will proceed] after consulting with your Sagacity. Concerning the columns and marbles of whatever kind you consider to be most precious and serviceable, please inform us yourself in writing . . . so that we may learn from your letter what quantity and what kind are needed, and that these may be conveyed from every quarter; for it is fitting that the most wondrous place in the world should be adorned according to its worth. As for the vault . . . if it is to be coffered, it may also be adorned with gold.[4]

Bishop Macarius made no objections to these elaborate plans. Indeed, he seized upon them as appropriate and accepted as well, without question, his own role as local supervisor of the construction and holder of the building once completed. In this regard he was in step with his fellow bishops in the empire who even this early were undertaking on their own the construction of ecclesiastical buildings and the furnishing of them on a truly impressive scale. As Eugenius, a contemporary of Constantine and bishop of Laodicea Combusta in Lycaonia, was described on his epitaph: "I was made bishop by the will of Almighty God, and I governed the bishopric with much merit for a full twenty-five years, and I rebuilt the whole church from its foundations with all the adornments around it, namely the porticoes, the atrium, the paintings, the mosaics, the water-fountain, the porch, and all the works of the stone-masons."[5]

The bishops moved into this role with what might seem surprising ease, despite the fact that in the New Testament scarce warrant can be found for it. It was, rather, their *paideia* that had trained them precisely for undertaking great building projects for the public weal. The spatial needs of the Christian communities provided the stimulus and warrant.

Although the details varied, by the fourth century the basic structure of the mass was set and observed throughout the empire.

Considerable space was needed to accommodate the large numbers present. As early as 250 the population of Asia Minor was becoming ever more Christian, and the congregation in Rome numbered in the very many thousands. By the early fourth century these numbers had increased almost exponentially. The community also required large buildings because the liturgy itself had evolved to require space for processions and other movements. Rooms were needed for storing the liturgical books and the sacred vessels and vestments.

Baptism, the other rite integral to Christian self-understanding and the sacrament that initiated newcomers into the community, was by this time increasingly administered at a solemn ceremony at the end of the Great Week or Holy Week that culminated in Easter. This rite, too, required space. At least by the fourth century baptism was performed in separate buildings because of the nakedness of the candidates, and the baptistries contained pools that were set into the floor.

Besides their cathedral complexes Christians built another impressive religious edifice, the martyrs' shrines. From the beginning they showed special reverence for the sites where their martyrs were buried, which included gathering there for prayers and ritual meals. By the middle of the second century they were constructing buildings in these places to shelter their gatherings and to show respect for the dead. In their simplest form these structures were not much more than a niche under an umbrella, like the *aedicula* honoring St. Peter that was uncovered in the middle of the twentieth century under St. Peter's basilica in Rome. These were the *martyria,* the Christian counterpart to the pagan *heroa.* In time Christians wanted to be buried near their martyrs, so they built more elaborate structures, which developed into both sanctuaries and mausolea, as well as goals of pilgrimage.

For their churches Christians even in the third century turned to what was at hand, the basilica. But they were able to take the definitive step only after 313, that fateful date when Constantine not only lifted the new religion to a preferred social and political status but also acted as the great catalyst for the development of a massive Christian material culture, strikingly accommodated to the material culture of the world over which he ruled. The significance of Constantine in the evolution of the relationship of Athens to Jerusalem in the area of architecture and the arts is difficult to exaggerate. The emperor set in motion a massive redefinition of space, indeed, redefinition of urban landscape, with the concomitant and inevitable redefinition of Christians' relationship to the material culture of Late Antiquity.

In function the basilica was just a large meeting hall used for official or semi-official functions, or at least open to general civic uses. Thus it could in theory be constructed according to a central plan, and it showed itself remarkably adaptive, especially in its Christian forms. But in the fourth century it was usually a longitudinal hall without aisles, covered with a timber roof, and terminating with a raised apse, which thus dominated it. This is the form Constantine followed in Rome for the great basilicas of the Lateran, of St. Peter, St. Paul, and St. Lawrence, and for others elsewhere. In its Christian forms one entered not from the side, as was otherwise the custom, but from the end opposite the apse, so that one's gaze was immediately directed to the altar and the bishop's *cathedra.*

Christians took an existing Roman form and adapted it for their purposes. But as Christians changed the form, the form also changed them, their worship, and their relationship to the material culture in which they lived their lives. With the emperor leading the way, Christians became almost overnight the greatest builders of public edifices in the empire. Most of these buildings were large, some of them of stunningly immense proportions. The basilica Constantine constructed in the Vatican sector of Rome over the supposed site of St. Peter's burial was longer than an American football field, with proportionate width. Essentially completed by 329, this very special *martyrium* could hold three thousand pilgrims.

Other ecclesiastical builders elsewhere followed the emperor's lead in trying to accommodate the crowds for Sunday worship or those who came on pilgrimage to the martyrs' shrines. Expense was not spared in any of these endeavors, which argues for considerable wealth in the Christian community even when the buildings were financed by the emperor. Further embellishment and adornment might continue for decades. No source suggests that all this activity and expense was an imposition from above on an unwilling Christian proletariat. Sources suggest, on the contrary, that ordinary folk entered with gusto into the enterprise when occasion offered. In the early fourth century when the time came for Bishop Porphyry of Gaza to excavate the foundations of his cathedral, "he made a prayer and a genuflection, and then he commanded the people to dig. Straightaway all of them, in unison of spirit and zeal, began to dig crying out 'Christ has won!' . . . And so in a few days all the places of the foundations were dug out and cleared."[6]

Constantine had set a high standard, as he indicated in his letter telling the bishops who had gathered to plan a church at Mambre to make it "worthy of my generosity and worthy of the Catholic and apostolic church."[7] The interiors of the Constantinian churches were utterly lavish in their outfitting, absorbing the panoply of architectural vocabulary proper to imperial palaces—gilded ceilings, gold and silver vessels and other furnishings, mosaic decorations, and variegated columns of polished marble. The emperor's first donation to the Lateran basilica alone consisted in 4,390 *solidi* for the purchase of lamps, 82 kilograms of gold for liturgical vessels, and 775 kilograms of silver. Within an amazingly short time, therefore, the interior of churches in at least the major centers of the empire began to glitter with the precious metals and mosaics that adorned them and with the jewels inset into the sacred vessels and furnishings, "like a queen escorted by her attendants," said Eusebius of the church at Tyre.[8]

These monumental structures with their truly palatial decorations made inevitable a more formal, elaborate, and highly ritualized service. They promoted further distinction in the sacred action between clergy and laity, with separate places for them in the church more clearly designated and with differentiation of roles more clearly emerging. Even so, their great space, augmented often by an exterior courtyard before the entrance as well as by other buildings adjacent or attached, encouraged procession, an impressive ritual movement in which clergy and laity alike took part. The great edifices changed the scale of everything, and the greater scale encouraged ever more elaborate performance.

Regular Sunday service in cathedrals began with the solemn entrance of the bishop and his clergy, often preceded by the people. After the first part of the service, the people moved from the nave to the altar and then back again in the offering of the gifts of bread and wine. Toward the end of the mass the congregation proceeded to the altar to receive the Eucharist. In major cities with special shrines, like Jerusalem, Constantinople, and Rome, the processions on occasion took to the streets of the cities, linking the churches to one another and especially to the cathedral, in a religious redefinition of the urban landscape. A physically Christian city resulted. The Christians' public rituals displaced and then replaced the older, official pagan rites and began to perform the same political function of upholding the structures of society.

As church rituals became more formalized and the walls and furnishings richer, both clergy and people asked for explanations of what the services meant. No theological interpretation of the Eucharist survives from the pre-Constantinian church, almost certainly because the issue was not urgent. Hearing the word of God read, engaging in the liturgical movements, and partaking of the bread and wine, as Jesus commanded, were sufficient. These actions united Christians with the Lord and strengthened them in the trials and tribulations of their lives. The action of receiving the Eucharist made Christ present among them in a special way and brought to their minds the events of his earlier physical life. This much they could gather from the different versions of the great Eucharistic prayer that had now assumed stable forms.

After Constantine, however, with more people involved in a public way in more elaborate ceremonies, formal explanations needed to be made. Preachers resorted to allegorical and mystical interpretations, which is perhaps the best that can be done for "a dance," an action where meaning was conveyed in gesture, in movement, in costume, and in highly ritualized words. Physical and visual elements transported those present to an altogether different reality. Like play the celebration lifted participants for the moment out of the "real world." Unlike play, however, it intended to put them in a world far more real and far more sublime than anything they otherwise experienced.

In fourth-century Milan on Holy Saturday Ambrose solemnly administered baptism to catechumens. The ritual began, symbolically, outside the baptistry. There Ambrose touched the ears and mouth of the catechumens to open them to faith and piety. Then their whole body was anointed with olive oil to make these new athletes of Christ ready for the struggle with Satan. When they entered the building they saw Ambrose consecrating the baptismal waters by tracing the sign of the cross on them and plunging into them his episcopal staff, sign of the shepherd he was. After the catechumens were stripped of their garments, they entered the font, where they were immersed three times in commemoration of Christ's three days in the tomb. Their emergence from the font symbolized Christ's resurrection from the tomb and their resurrection from their old way of life. After the oil of chrism was poured on their heads, Ambrose washed their feet in imitation of Christ at the Last Supper. They were then clothed in fresh white garments, signs that they had "put on Christ," after which Ambrose traced the sign of the cross on their foreheads and embraced them as a liturgical gesture of peace and welcome.

The altar, the central piece of church furniture—what was it in ritual reality? It was many things, all at once—table set for a meal, altar for sacrifice, tomb of Christ, the body of Christ, tomb of the martyr whose relics it contains (for within a relatively short time this practice spread and became normative), the throne of God, the table of the Law, the table of the manna in the desert. All these things and possibly more. The altar was therefore kissed, it was incensed and covered with precious linens. It held a golden cup and dish, and it was flooded with light by lamps and candles.

The following text, attributed to St. Germanus, patriarch of Constantinople, is from the late seventh century and describes the Byzantine liturgy, but it indicates a reality that became pervasive much earlier in both East and West. It says of the altar:

> The holy table is the place where Christ was buried, and on which is set forth the true bread from heaven, the mystic and bloodless sacrifice, i.e., Christ . . . It is also the throne upon which God, who is borne up by the cherubim, has rested. At this table, too, Christ sat down at his last supper in the midst of his apostles and, taking bread and wine, said to them, "Take, eat and drink of it: this is my body and blood." It was prefigured by the table of the Law on which was the manna that comes down from heaven.[9]

What was the church building itself? We do not have to wait for the elaborate allegories of Byzantium to know that it was understood as the new Jerusalem and the earthly replica of the heavenly court. As Gregory the Great put it: "Can any of the faithful doubt that at the hour of the Eucharistic sacrifice the heavens open at the priest's calling, that in this mystery of Jesus Christ the choirs of angels are present, the heights joined to the depths, earth linked with heaven, the visible united with the invisible?"[10]

As the ceremony for the consecration of a church evolved, it became a kind of baptism for the building, which represents the body of Christ, that is, the assembly of the faithful. The richness of imagery corresponded to the increasing richness of church interiors and the vastness of their space, which in turn argued to the more conspicuous wealth of at least many members of the Christian community and their accommodation to the new state of affairs.

The flight of some Christians "to the desert" during the fourth century indicated that not all were happy with what was happening to their religion—or at least to their coreligionists, whom they perceived as too at ease with the ways of the world and too far removed from the prophetic stance of the martyrs. By their action these ascetics raised a silent voice of protest against a materialism that might seem to be manifested even in liturgical developments, but they were the voice of a minority. Most Christians from every social class and in every part of the empire seem to have glided into this change without scruple. They did so because the world in which they lived was fundamentally an illiterate one and therefore a world of statuary, public ritual, and public spectacles, a world in which meaning was most widely diffused visually.

In their attempt to ingratiate Christianity with the intellectuals of their day, the Apologists argued that their "philosophy," like that of their fellow philosophers who were not Christians, considered absurd the idea that the divinity could be seen, and therefore absurd that it could be depicted. In this context the philosophical arguments weighed more heavily, it seems, than Israel's prohibition of graven images. The Apologists presented themselves as theistic philosophers, dedicated to the highest ideals of ethics and worship, unlike their enemies, who were depraved and disgustingly ignorant fools. At the turn of the third century Clement of Alexandria, influenced by Platonism, would go further and denigrate art as a lie, for a painted plant is not a real plant—and Christians surely do not worship images.

Yet all these authors wrote and spoke in order to give Christianity, still a relatively obscure sect, a more public and visible form. The caution or disdain some of them expressed toward the figurative arts corresponds to the lack of material evidence of such art among Christians until the third century. Although this dearth might seem to substantiate the claim that the Apologists' arguments were in these early times shared by their coreligionists, it is better explained by Christians' lack of land and capital, which began to change considerably about the year 200. With more Christians having more money they began to express their religion by using the material forms they saw all around them.

Just as the educated among them saw no problem in studying philosophy from a pagan, or in taking Virgil and Cicero as their models of eloquence, Christians who had the means saw no problem with depictions of biblical scenes and, soon, depictions of Christ. The principle that the invisible God could not and should not be depicted held for a long time, but Christ, it was argued, was not invisible, for he had lived among us as a human being. Symbolic representations of him as the Good Shepherd, which made no pretense at being a real likeness, posed even less of a problem.

Even if Christians in the first two centuries observed a taboo regarding representations of biblical scenes and personages, they had largely discarded it as early as the middle of the third century. True, voices would continue to be raised in protest or scruple, sometimes by the highest authority. Around A.D. 306, Canon 36 of the important Council of Elvira in Spain, for instance, absolutely prohibited the use of pictures in churches: "There should be no pictures in the church building lest what is worshiped and adored might be painted on the walls."[11] Bishops even after Constantine occasionally showed themselves, if not altogether negative, surely reserved on the issue, fearing it smacked of idolatry or of paganism. In the eighth and ninth centuries these texts would be mustered to good effect in the East to support the Iconoclast cause, and they lay ready to be hauled out in the West for similar causes at later times.

Not until the Iconoclast period, however, did these voices seriously dampen the enterprise in East or West. Other voices were singing another tune: the mosaics and frescos brought delight to the spirit and raised it to God; they enhanced the beauty and grandeur of the Lord's temples; they illumined with instruction the minds of all Christians and spurred their souls to the pursuit of holiness. Eusebius himself, who made clear to Constantine that attempts to paint portraits of Christ were badly misguided, praised him for the other religious images he placed in his new capital of Constantinople, including images of the Good Shepherd, "familiar to those who have a grounding in Holy Scripture," and of Daniel with the lions. A few decades later Gregory, bishop of Nyssa, tells how paintings of the sacrifice of Isaac, which he had "often seen," did not fail to bring tears to his eyes. After him St. Nilus, bishop of Ancyra, calls for "filling the holy church with pictures from the Old and New Testaments, executed by an excellent painter," for they instruct the illiterate and rouse them to emulate the glorious feats depicted.[12]

This verbal testimony, by no means unanimous but still impressive in conveying the enthusiasm for artistic representations of biblical scenes and of saints and martyrs, seems inadequate in comparison with the quantity and quality of the visual evidence that has survived. In the West such images include the great fourth-century mosaic in the apse of Santa Pudentiana in Rome depicting Christ on a throne with a book in his hand, surrounded by the Apostles and by saints Pudentiana and Praxedes; the thirty-six mosaic panels from the fifth century in Santa Maria Maggiore in Rome notable for depictions of scenes and personages from the Old Testament, including Abraham, Isaac, Jacob, Moses, and Joshua; and, most stunning, the monumental grandeur of the exquisite and seemingly countless series of mosaics from the fifth and sixth centuries in the churches and baptistries of Ravenna.

Although for himself Augustine, the sensualist, feared the beauty artists produced because, if captivated by it, he would not be able to move beyond it to its source, Beauty itself, his words reveal the sensitivity to the beautiful that other refined Romans felt: "O my God, my Glory, for these things too I offer you a hymn of thanksgiving. I make a sacrifice of praise to him who sanctifies me, for the beauty that flows through artists' souls and thence into their skillful hands comes from the Beauty that is above their souls and for which my soul sighs all through the day and all through the night."[13]

Though ambivalent as usual about pleasure that comes from the senses, Augustine still tells of "the tears I shed on hearing the songs of the church," and speaks of his pleasure at "all the melody of those lovely chants to which the Psalms of David are habitually sung."[14] Hymns and canticles to the Lord were so enthusiastically described in the Scriptures that Christians seem to have been even less reserved about music than about other aspects of culture four. From the earliest times they gathered on a daily basis for prayer in the morning and evening that consisted largely in the psalms. Morning prayer developed into a service of praise that included the "praise" psalms, that is, psalms 148–150, so that the service itself became known as Lauds. The evening service became known, appropriately, as Vespers. At a certain point both services were put to music.

The attitude of Christians toward the artistic culture of their ambiance is perhaps best revealed by the respect they showed toward statues of the pagan gods. The *paideia* in which their leaders had been trained as boys inculcated tolerance with a view to the good of the commonwealth. The best evidence of their tolerance is the large number of pagan statues that have survived despite the devastations of war and plunder. Yes, Christians sometimes smashed them to pieces and boasted of it, but most seem to have been remarkably insouciant toward these manifestations of a religion they thought inadequate and in irreversible decline. The Christian matron Marina set up a splendid gallery of pagan statues in her palace, which she certainly did not do because it helped her devotion. Her action prompted the sarcastic observation by a non-Christian, "The inhabitants of Olympus, having converted, live here undisturbed."[15]

From the Iconoclast Controversy to the Renaissance

By the sixth century icons had proliferated, especially in the East. Icons are not simply certain sacred images whose type we easily recognize but sacred images to which are shown special marks of veneration, like bowing, incensing, and kissing. Although such forms of veneration were practiced in the West, they were much more prevalent, with more importance attached to them, in the East. Icons were found in churches, of course, but also in other public spaces as well as in private homes.

The Iconoclast controversy broke out in Constantinople in 726 and lasted for well over a century. A complicated and bitter affair, it was closely tied to the declining political and cultural fortunes of the Eastern empire as it entered its own "Dark Ages." By and large the major protagonists on the Iconoclast side were the emperors themselves, beginning with Leo III. They saw their political and military reverses as a punishment from God for the sin of idolatry committed by the cult of images. Iconoclasm was thus a top-down movement, but the leaders were obviously able to gather support from below.

Apologists for the Iconoclast position of course repudiated what they saw as idolatry, but some of them also had philosophical and theological arguments against sacred images as such. Moderates among them might tolerate images for didactic reasons, as books for the illiterate, but then if that is the only function images perform, they by definition cease to be icons. The Iconoclasts' opposition to images was further fired by the attribution of miracles to them.

Just how much actual image-smashing occurred during the long Iconoclast period is not known, but occur it did, with the stripping of mosaics and frescoes from churches, the destruction or expropriation of altars and church furnishings, the burning of relics, and the destruction of icons outside church precincts.

The controversy spilled over into the West on the highest level, bringing Charlemagne and Pope Hadrian I into disagreement. In Italy word of the controversy was also spread to lower levels of clergy and the laity by refugees escaping the persecution. The Carolingian court for its part produced the *Libri Carolini,* a refutation of the Iconophile decrees of the Second Council of Nicaea, 787. Since only a few copies of the *Libri* were made at the time, it had scant circulation and virtually no influence until it was reclaimed in the sixteenth century by Protestant reformers.

Despite the interest of the Frankish court in the matter and the active role the papacy, especially Hadrian I, took in the controversy, during the Middle Ages the veneration of images remained a peripheral and fundamentally uncontested issue in the West. The Waldensians and the Cathars opposed the practice in the thirteenth century, as did Wycliffe and Hus in the fourteen and fifteenth. Yet even for them images were symptoms of the deeper problems on which their attention was really focused. The *Libri Carolini* was thus of more importance in the sixteenth century than it was in the eighth and ninth. Nonetheless, Pope Hadrian's enthusiastic approval of the decree of the Second Council of Nicaea in 787, which declared the veneration of images a holy and orthodox practice, provided at the highest level an official stance, solemnly pronounced by an Eastern council the papacy recognized as ecumenical, that would henceforth remain basically unchanged.

When the council was convoked, Hadrian sent two envoys with a letter in which he stoutly maintained that veneration of images was traditional and orthodox, and he cited a number of patristic witnesses to the fact. He was surely further confirmed in his viewpoint because at that very time a new phase of church building had recently begun in Rome, with impressive mosaics of Christ and the saints. His letter was enthusiastically received at the council, and to his envoys were extended signs of the greatest respect.

Drawn up with much care in the Roman Curia, Hadrian's letter spoke of "honoring" and "venerating" images, not "adoring" them. It then exhorted bishops "to paint in the churches the representations of divine history to recall the work of our salvation, as well as to teach the ignorant . . . and to set in the dwelling-place of God the holy image of our Lord in his incarnate human form" along with those of Mary, the apostles, martyrs, and confessors, "whom we venerate when, out of love for them, we represent them in painting." The letter explained what the object of veneration was in images of Christ: "By means of a visible face, our spirit is carried away by a spiritual attraction towards the invisible majesty of the divinity by contemplating the image in which is represented the flesh that the Son of God deigned to take for our salvation. Let us then adore and praise this Redeemer of ours, glorifying him in spirit, for, as it is written, 'God is spirit.'"[16]

The decree of the council itself is several paragraphs long and repeats ideas found in Hadrian's letter. For both Hadrian and the council the Incarnation justified pictorial representations of Christ. The decree emphasized that the veneration of images was traditional and helpful, that sacred images of Christ make more vivid his humanity, that the honor paid the image transverses it to reach the model, and that the veneration of an image is not the same thing as the adoration paid to Christ; rather, it resembles the veneration shown to the books of the Gospel and the images of the cross. The decree enjoined, further, that these sacred images, "whether painted or made of mosaic, or of other suitable material, are to be exposed in the holy churches of God, on sacred instruments and vestments, on walls and panels, in houses and in public streets."[17]

The council was an important but transitory victory for the Iconophile party. The controversy broke out again in 814 under Emperor Leo V and dragged on in the East for another half-century. The final outcome was a triumph for the Iconophiles in that it established the central position of icons in the worship and devotion of all the Orthodox communions. What this meant for them on the deepest level was that God, who is holy by nature, is present as a deifying energy in all human saints and as a sanctifying energy in their relics and images. Although their opponents made an exception for the Eucharist, they held that the immense gulf between the transcendent and the created could not be bridged, an argument altogether consonant with culture one.

The struggle generated among the Iconophiles an impressive body of literature in defense of their position. During the long controversy, the arguments both sides produced were not particularly original, but they were now formulated in a stronger, more developed, and better-focused way. Icons, indeed sacred images as such, had become politicized. They had become the object of open and often violent confrontation. This forced into front and center an issue that had lurked in the background and on the periphery of Christian reflection, an issue often mentioned merely in passing, not pursued in depth. That now changed.

John of Damascus (Damascene) was the most important and influential thinker to formulate the case for the icon, and his three Orations on the subject composed in the early eighth century form the first Christian treatise devoted explicitly and exclusively to sacred images. The work was known and studied in Rome long before Hadrian composed his letter. But Damascene was not alone in making this period the richest in literature on the subject, which sometimes takes the authors into the profoundest aspects of Christology. The participants in the Second Council of Nicaea brought the fruits of this reflection with them to the council. When Protestant Iconoclasm broke out in the West many centuries later, Catholics had classic texts on hand to deal with it, which perhaps made their task too facile and resulted for the most part in their just repeating the now standard arguments.

In the West, meanwhile, the Frankish court of Charlemagne and his son Louis the Pious continued to have reservations about the decree of Second Nicaea, of which it had only a hasty and defective Latin translation. The bishops and theologians influential at the court held to a simply didactic function for images, for which they invoked especially the authority of Gregory the Great. Opposed, therefore, to the destruction of images, they wanted to steer a midway course between Iconoclasm and their understanding of the "veneration" sanctioned at the council.

In his reply to Charlemagne Pope Hadrian informed the emperor that the custom in Rome "has been always first to anoint sacred images and paintings with holy chrism before giving them over to be venerated by the faithful." He described the great paintings and mosaics in the Roman churches executed at the order or at least with the encouragement of many popes. He concluded his description of each pontificate with the refrain "and we still venerate these sacred images today."[18]

With the breakup of the Carolingian empire after the death of Louis the Pious and then the destructive incursions of the Norsemen, Magyars, and Saracens into much of Western Europe, the memory of a matter that the Frankish court had always considered of secondary importance evaporated. In the differing viewpoints between Rome and the Franks, it is tempting to see an anticipation of a fundamental difference in religious personality between northern Europe and the Mediterranean world that would surface definitively only in the sixteenth century. But it is perhaps more accurate to see the difference as another manifestation of how a bookish culture like that of the authors of the Carolingian documents can hardly help from turning art and performance into the equivalent of a book, into a repository of ideas and teachings.

The papacy was meanwhile about to plunge into perhaps its most unsettled and morally sordid period, which pushed out of memory the high theological arguments generated by the Iconoclast controversy. What survived in Rome and elsewhere were the images themselves. What also survived were the rituals of bowing before the images, kissing them, carrying them in procession, or simply praying in front of them, whether in church or in some other place. In the West the icon as such never became part of the official liturgy of the church, but sacred images evoked certain actions that were highly stylized and that resembled, in that sense, somebody performing a ritual role.

Meanwhile in the West the impulse to build, to sculpt, and to paint continued even during the most troubled centuries of the early Middle Ages. Monastic communities, those oases of order in a bellicose world, were once again crucial. Charlemagne was able to capitalize on this reality for the extensive building campaigns he promoted, but architecture was just a part of the material phenomenon that produced illuminated manuscripts, goldwork and enameling, ivory carving, and gem engraving whose quality has in some ways never been equaled. Most of this production was religious in character and much of it destined for liturgical use. The architects and artisans behind it did not learn their skills or acquire their almost infallibly good taste in school. Few were literate.

As Europe in the eleventh century began to recover from the

many travails of the previous century, when it had been subjected to brigandage from within and without, these architects and artisans reappeared, almost miraculously, it seems, and a building enthusiasm once again caught Christian leaders. In this still radically rural society in which the revival of cities was just on the horizon, the monasteries that dotted the countryside were enlarged or restored after many decades of plundering and devastation, and new ones were built. In the tenth and eleventh centuries the monastery of Cluny, which would eventually have hundreds of dependent houses spread across Europe, emerged as the dominant religious institution of the age.

Even though their monastery was tucked away in the forests of Burgundy, the abbots of Cluny never thought of themselves as recluses withdrawn from the world and its concerns. While devoted to the liturgical life of their monastery and promoters of a more disciplined clerical life, they were far from being exemplars of culture one. The excellent St. Odilo boasted that he had found the monastery wood and left it marble. His equally impressive successor, St Hugh, abbot from 1049 to 1109, undertook in 1088 to rebuild the monastery church, which when it was finally completed about a half-century later was the largest in Christendom, 555 feet long, bigger than the basilica of St. Peter in Rome.

In the twelfth century the powerful Suger, abbot of the royal abbey of St. Denis outside Paris, left a detailed account of the art treasures the abbey church contained, giving a good idea of how elaborate the decoration was. In the account he revealed that this material culture carried him to another world, an experience that somewhat echoes that of the envoys of Prince Vladimir. Suger said that his "delight in the beauty of the house of God" led him to "see myself dwelling, as it were, in some strange region of the universe that neither exists entirely in the slime of the earth nor entirely in the purity of heaven; and I see that, by the grace of God, I can be transported from this inferior to that higher world." Or, as he says in a poem he composed about the central west portal of the church:

> Bright is the noble work; but, being nobly bright, the work
> Should brighten the minds so that they may travel, through the true lights,
> To the True Light where Christ is the true door.[19]

But it was with the revival of the cities, so noticeable by the twelfth century, that the great cathedrals and other churches began to appear in notable number, either as replacements of earlier structures or as new edifices where nothing had existed before. Besides cathedrals there were parish churches, the urban monasteries of canons like the Victorines and the Premonstratensians, and then the great collegiate churches of the mendicant orders, which include some of Europe's most famous buildings, like the Franciscan church of Santa Croce and the Dominican church of Santa Maria Novella in Florence. There were, further, the manor chapels, the churches at pilgrims' shrines, and the oratories of the confraternities. These places of worship were for the most part richly, even gaudily, decorated either with mosaics or, increasingly, with frescoes.

The creation of these monuments cannot be attributed simply to an ongoing impetus from earlier centuries; nor can we say that the motivation for them was strictly religious, whatever that might mean in context. Cities were built at an extraordinarily rapid pace, and the ecclesiastical buildings were part of a larger and contagious enthusiasm. Urban pride played a huge role in the enterprise, and as the patronage of rich and powerful individuals began to be more operative toward the end of the period, so did family pride and the enhancement of the patron's prestige.

Voices were raised urging restraint, urging simplicity and austerity, among them the Cistercians' in the twelfth century. Bernard, whose religious language was, as we have seen, often blatantly sensual, expressed disdain for the artistic elegance of Cluny. Monks as truly spiritual persons, he pointed out, had transcended the need for such material crutches. Yet even the Cistercians built churches beautiful in their very austerity, and their attitude, important though it was, did not represent the mainstream.

The Franciscans in the following century raised voluntary poverty to a centrality in Christian ideals that it had never had before and, moreover, extended it in new and radical ways beyond the individual friar to the corporation, the order itself. This led to furious dissensions and even schisms within the order, beginning with the bitter controversy over the construction of the basilica in Assisi in honor of Francis. Over the objections of many of the friars, the basilica was built under Franciscan auspices and was soon decorated with magnificent frescoes by Simone Martini, Giotto (or pseudo-Giotto), and others.

The Franciscan ideal of corporate poverty affected the other mendicant orders founded in the thirteenth century, with similar results. Whatever poverty meant for these groups, however, it did not preclude building churches on a grand scale and enhancing them with the most exquisite works of art available. In the early sixteenth century, for instance, Egidio da Viterbo became prior general of the Augustinians and undertook a reform of them. The Augustinians were members of a mendicant order founded in the thirteenth century out of various congregations of Italian hermits and, as mendicants, were influenced by the Franciscan tradition. In Egidio's eyes the eremitical heritage only intensified the mendicant emphasis on poverty that he tried to enforce within the order. But for him as for most others this poverty was an issue quite separate from what was appropriate for churches. Egidio lived in Rome during the pontificate of Pope Julius II, who, with Bramante as his architect, took the first steps in constructing the new basilica of

St. Peter. For that undertaking Egidio had nothing but praise, enthusiastically extolling the idea of raising the new church "up to the very heavens." Let it soar to be "a most magnificent edifice, that God might be more magnificently praised."[20]

Egidio's Rome was also the Rome of Raphael and Michelangelo, Rome of the Renaissance. Mention of their names is sufficient to put into focus the tremendous production of sculpture and painting, much of it religious, that characterized Western Europe and especially Italy in the fifteenth and early sixteenth centuries. The phenomenon was also verified, however, outside the realm of high art, in small churches as well as great. In 1488 a country church in Norfolk "had lamps burning not only before the Rood with Mary and John, and an image of the Trinity, but before a separate statue of the Virgin, and images of Saints Margaret, Anne, Nicholas, John the Baptist, Thomas Becket, Christopher, Erasmus, James the Great, Katherine, Petronella, Sythe, and Michael the Archangel. . . . a very characteristic late-medieval list."[21]

Frescoes continued to be painted on the walls, ceilings, and apses of churches and chapels, as in the Sistine Chapel, but there was now a proliferation of tempera and oil paintings as altar pieces for the many secondary altars in churches. The quantity was enormous, especially in central Italy, as the devout, the self-referential, and the self-referentially devout vied with one other as patrons in the adornment of family chapels, favorite shrines, and even dormitory rooms, such those painted by Fra Angelico in the convent of San Marco, Florence. Under the influence of the humanist movement, painters began exploring mythological subjects, which were sometimes justified through allegorical interpretations but sometimes not justified at all. They were painted simply for the beauty and delight of it. The nude, relatively rare in the Middle Ages, reappeared—for saints, as in Michelangelo's David, and even for Christ himself, as in his Risen Christ in the church of Santa Maria sopra Minerva in Rome.

The mass and sacraments celebrated in various kinds of sacred edifices retained basic elements that were well established by the sixth century. Some aspects of those elements took on a different significance, however, because the social context had changed. Latin, the language of the Roman liturgy, had become increasingly incomprehensible to an ever larger percentage of the population. The original significance of gestures and symbols had also become obscure, subject to far-fetched interpretations, as they became detached in time and place from their origins. This situation further promoted allegorical interpretations of the liturgical action, as well as of the altar, the church furnishings, and the building itself.

William Durandus was an important thirteenth-century canonist and legal official at the papal court whose *Rationale Divinorum Officiorum* is filled with such interpretations. No aspect is too great or too small to escape his symbolic imagination. In describing how a church is to be built, he shows how the building is more than a building, "for the material church, wherein the people assemble to set forth God's holy praise, symbolizes that holy church that is built in Heaven with living stones." He then describes the significance of elements of the material church, beginning with the walls: "The faithful predestined to eternal life are the stones in the structure of this wall, which shall be continually built up until the end of the world. One stone is added to another . . . and whoever in Holy Church undertakes painful labors from brotherly love, he bears up the weight of the stones placed above him. The stones of larger size placed on the outside and angles of the building are persons of holier life than others; by their merits and prayers they strengthen weaker brethren in Holy Church."[22]

Similar allegorical interpretations were devised for the mass itself, which was sometimes presented as a reenactment of the last days of Jesus' life, so that when the priest entered the sanctuary he symbolically represented Jesus entering the Garden of Gethsemane the night before he died, and so forth. Although part of the mentality of the age, such musings when applied to the mass indicate an incomprehension fostered by the fact that it was being celebrated in a language foreign to most laymen and even to a large number of priests. This does not necessarily mean that priests and people were less attached to the liturgy because of faulty or incorrect understanding, for culture four is not about understanding per se but about experience of art and performance. Nonetheless, this situation helped foster in the sixteenth century not only a determination among the Reformers to turn liturgies into the vernacular but also an animus against "ceremonies" that, according to them, were hardly distinguishable from magic.

But the mass, however understood or misunderstood, was only one piece of the liturgical scene that defined the day and, to a great extent, the lives of a large number of people. The celebration of the Liturgical Hours, important in Late Antiquity, took on an even greater importance in the Middle Ages. Cultivated by the monks, it later surged as an urban phenomenon through the cathedral clergy and through the canons regular like the Victorines in Paris. In the thirteenth century it was continued, sometimes in less elaborate form, by the Dominicans, Franciscans, and the other mendicant orders. The church that Durandus described, in other words, was far from being a building reserved simply for a Sunday service or even for masses during the week, all of which would be celebrated in the morning, usually early. It was a building in which, when a sufficient number of priests served it, the Hours were celebrated throughout the day.

Although the Hours was a clerical service, with no particular notice taken of any laity who might be present, it was consistently popular with the devout among them throughout the whole period. In the sixteenth century, for instance, the members of the newly formed Jesuit order eliminated from their daily regimen chanting or reciting the Hours in common, a major departure from tradition for a religious order. This meant that in their churches not even Vespers would be provided, much less sung Vespers. Despite this provision, they found that they could not resist the demand from the laity for sung Vespers in particular. As the provincial superior of India reported to Ignatius of Loyola, the founder, about both Vespers and mass, "Sung liturgies were introduced into our college because there was no hope of doing otherwise, so great is the people's attachment to them."[23] At that same time the provincial from Bahia in far-away Brazil reported that three different choirs were in operation for Vespers on Sundays and feast days—one accompanied with organ, another with clavichord, the third with flutes.

Music for religious purposes was not contained within the boundaries of mass and the Hours, and especially in later centuries it could be elaborate indeed. The text of religious plays, for instance, was sung, whether these were more or less successfully knitted into the fabric of the mass, as with the *Quem quaeritis* Easter dialogue, or simply performed in the context of the liturgy, as in the Magi plays. The Magi plays involved at least thirteen characters, who acted out their parts as they sang them, which required movement that resembled in its effect a liturgical procession.

Processions through city streets, prominent at least in certain locations in Christian antiquity, were an important part of the urban ritual in the Middle Ages. Religious feast days provided most of the occasions for such communitarian performances, which were a complex mixture of devotion, civic pride, and manifestation of social stratification. Music was integral to them.

Different cities honored their patrons on their feast days, on the so-called Rogation Days imploring help for a good harvest, which required processions into the fields, and on other occasions. Special events required music, which got more elaborate as the centuries rolled on. In India in 1558, for instance, a mass to open the academic year at the Jesuit college was celebrated with shawns, kettledrums, trumpets, flutes, and violins, and the same instruments were used after mass in a procession through the streets.

By the end of the Middle Ages, the early summer feast of Corpus Christi was observed with an elaborate procession in almost every city, town, and hamlet of Western Europe. The procession dominated the day. Preparations were extensive—flowers for children to strew along the long route had to be procured, banners made, candles and torches purchased, rich vestments and other outfits got ready, singers and bell ringers hired. The procession with the Eucharistic host stopped along the way at numerous places important to the locality, which could include bridges, mills, even trees, as well as chapels, shrines, and other sites of special devotion.

The hymns from the official liturgy of the day, whose wording is attributed to Thomas Aquinas, were not originally intended for processions but were easily adapted to them and almost universally used, especially the *Pange, lingua,* with its suitable trochaic mode. Other chants and hymns, some borrowed from different feasts, were sung almost continuously as the procession wended its way along the route. In some Catholic countries the celebration of the feast has continued, often in even more elaborate forms, up to the present.

The Great Crisis

In the West the great crisis came crashing down upon culture four in the sixteenth century. The attack was aimed at its religious aspects under the rubrics of "ceremonies" and "idolatry," but it had repercussions beyond the sacred. A significant shift in religious and aesthetic sensibilities in certain segments of the population in certain parts of Europe set the stage for the crisis and would continue long after it ended.

The other three cultures, though now in open warfare among themselves, ganged up on culture four, resulting in a convergence that erupted in sometimes ferocious efforts to force it to conform to their own systems. The prophets from culture one attacked it for its profanation of the transcendent. The crisis provided new occasion for the academics of culture two to reduce it to ideas. Culture three, to whose poetic language culture four had recourse when forced to put itself into words, showed restraint, but in Erasmus, its most influential spokesman, it manifested the less irenic side of its character and betrayed the repugnance of the *paideia,* as he understood it, for excess and irrationality.

Devout circles in the fifteenth century showed a new appreciation for an interiorized, even mystical religious experience over external performance. The *Imitation of Christ,* in circulation early in the century, quickly became popular, and the call it issued in the very first chapter "to withdraw thy heart from the love of visible things and turn thyself to things invisible," traditional though it was, took on a new urgency and had a wider appeal than previously. In the late Middle Ages many people felt that religion lavished too much of its attention on the visible and tangible, which, moreover, took forms they considered exaggerated, bizarre, and "superstitious."

The invention of printing was a great boost to the other three cultures, but except for music, its ultimate impact on four was ambivalent. It made for easy dissemination of woodcuts and engravings, which became new art forms in themselves. Yet it subtly promoted the persuasion that meaning could be conveyed better in word than in gesture, better in print than in procession, better in concept than in image. It was surely a catalyst in the war against "ignorance and superstition" that both Protestants and Catholics would wage with such vigor in the sixteenth century, but ignorance and superstition were often code words for "idolatry and ceremonies." For sixteenth-century reformers of "ceremonies," correct understanding was the prerequisite to acceptable participation in worship. To turn Martha Graham's words around, you had to be able to define it before you could dance it.

Resentment of clerical and ecclesiastical wealth received ever more widespread voice, just as concern for organized assistance to the marginalized elements of society grew. Judas' question, "Could this not have been sold and given to the poor?" was frequently asked, especially where church decoration and ritual stunned by their sumptuousness.

How to account, however, for the rage that gripped mobs of ordinary folk as they burst into churches and chapels to smash and hack to pieces objects they had until recently treated with reverence and devotion? Preachers had created and fanned indignation by telling them they had been duped into idolatry and their salvation jeopardized. On the obvious level that explains it. Yet the suspicion is well founded that the violence against the images (and their correlate, relics) was sideways anger, an expression of frustration at other grievances long festering—social, economic, political, and ecclesiastical—whose amelioration now seemed at hand. The preachers promised better days. To smash the images was to smash the status quo. In its very sensationalism the violence created the impression of a revolutionary leap forward.

Destroying objects was a way of settling old scores. In both Germany and Scotland Iconoclasts sometimes singled out images of St. Francis for particular contempt. In Zwickau in 1524 an image of the saint wearing ass's ears was set up in the town fountain and then burned. Similar incidents were later reported in Perth, Aberdeen, and elsewhere. Just why this occurred is not clear, but the saint might have stood, as far as intellectuals were concerned, for the stupidities of Scholastic theology and canon law. He might have stood for all the mendicant orders, whose begging the Reformers had discredited and whose pastoral practices they had derided. Wonderworking images were also objects of special contempt, sometimes because they were associated with witchcraft. Paintings of Mary were in mock fashion put on trial for sorcery and, when found guilty, burned.

Throughout his life Erasmus advocated simplicity and intelligibility in worship and campaigned relentlessly against what he considered the superstitions and excesses of medieval piety. He minimized the visible and material aspects of worship in favor of a more interiorized religion. Although this trait persisted throughout his life, it was stronger in his early years, as when in the *Handbook of the Christian Soldier* he pronounced that you can only establish perfect piety when you "progress from visible things . . . to the invisible."[24]

Among his lesser known works is a full liturgy he wrote for Our Lady of Loreto, that is, he wrote the prayers for the mass, selected the readings from the Bible, and composed a homily. He was therefore in no way interested in a refashioning of the traditional structure of the mass, but he harped on too much faith being put in "Judaizing ceremonies." In the sixteenth century, largely through Erasmus, the word *ceremoniae* acquired the pejorative meaning of "trivial little rituals," which he thought abounded everywhere. Erasmus also focused on services he thought too elaborate and sumptuous: "What is the use of so many baptistries, candelabra, gold statues? What is the good of the vastly expensive organs, as they call them? What is the good of that costly musical neighing when meanwhile our brothers and sisters, Christ's living temples, waste away in hunger and thirst?"[25]

Erasmus had some awareness of the *rinascita dell' arte* of the two hundred years since Giotto, and he evaluated it positively. But he betrayed its place in his hierarchy of values when he asserted that Pliny's *Natural History* was worth more than all the works of all the sculptors and painters Pliny refers to in it. Erasmus was certainly not an Iconoclast, but he campaigned so zealously for what he deemed the moral and intellectual correctness of paintings in churches and elsewhere that he makes the few words on the subject at the Council of Trent pale in comparison: "What shall I say about the licence so often found in statues and pictures? We see depicted and exposed to the eyes what would be disgraceful even to mention. . . . Why is it necessary to depict any old story in the churches? A young man and a girl lying in bed? David looking from a window at Bathsheba and luring her into adultery? Or the daughter of Herodias dancing? These subjects, it is true, are taken from the Scriptures, but when it comes to depictions of women how much naughtiness is admixed by the artists!"[26]

He worried that images of the saints not only distracted Christians from emulation of their virtues, the only correct aspect of their cult, but also seduced them into idolatry. As Folly puts it in *Praise of Folly,* "I am not so foolish as to petition painted stone images; they would only detract from my worship, since only stupid and unimaginative people worship these idols instead of the saints themselves. And the same thing would happen to me that happens to the saints—they are thrown out of doors by their substitutes."[27] What Folly says about the saints she could just as well say about depictions of Christ. The *Folly,* a sensational success, appeared in 1511, the eve of the Reformation. Once Protestant Iconoclasm broke out, Erasmus had to defend himself: "I have never condemned either the saints or their images but only superstition, that images be treated as if they were alive, and that folk should bow the head before them, fall on the ground, crawl on their knees, kiss and fondle the carvings."[28]

While he did not condemn the saints, he made light of their intercessory powers, which is often what their images made most vivid to their devotees. Although he believed that reading the New Testament rendered Christ more present than if he were seen with one's own eyes, he betrayed no inkling that a somewhat similar presence might be effected by an icon, as Greek theologians maintained. He was scandalized that painters violated his standards of decorum when they would lend the appearance of Apollo to Christ, not knowing that in the patristic era, so pure in Erasmus's view, Christ "wrested his most potent attributes" from the pagan gods.[29]

In this regard Erasmus differed altogether from Albrecht Dürer, whom he and his circle liked to call "the Apelles of our age." Dürer said: "Just as Greek and Roman authors attributed the most beautiful human shape to their false god, Apollo, so will we use the same proportions for Christ our Lord, who was the most beautiful man in the universe. And just as they employed Venus as the most beautiful woman, so will we chastely present the same lovely figure as the most pure Virgin Mary, the mother of God. Hercules we will transform into Samson, and with all the others we will do likewise."[30]

For the immediate future, however, it was Erasmus, not Dürer, who was the harbinger of things to come. The storm broke on January 27, 1522, when in Wittenberg Andreas Karlstadt published his strongest indictment of images, in which the opening line reads: "That we have images in churches and houses of God is wrong and contrary to the First Commandment: Thou shalt not have other gods." Images bring death to those who worship or venerate them: "Our churches can rightly be called murderers' caves, because in them our spirit is stricken and slain. It would be a thousand times more appropriate if these images were set up in hell or the fiery furnace than in the houses of God." Karlstadt denounced and dismissed the traditional arguments for images, including their didactic function: "Christ says, My sheep listen to my voice. He does not say, They see my image or the image of the saints."[31]

True prophet, Karlstadt pronounced judgment rather than argued or attempted to persuade. Basing his position exclusively on biblical texts, especially the prophets, he countenanced no compromise, no middle ground. Human customs must yield to divine ordinances: "Thou shalt not worship them. Thou shalt not venerate them. Thou shalt not kneel before them. Thou shalt not light a candle before them. God says: If I had wanted you to venerate me or my saints in pictures, I would not have forbidden you to make pictures and likenesses."[32]

Even before Karlstadt wrote he had helped convince the city council of Wittenberg to remove images from the churches, a decision Melanchthon objected to, as did Luther himself when he returned to the city about a month later. Luther annulled the ordinances, openly broke with Karlstadt, and began attacking him in print. Once again demonstrating how difficult it is to categorize him, Luther espoused a more moderate position—or perhaps positions, for his views changed over the years. If images were to be removed from churches, that was the duty of the proper authorities. Wanton destruction of them caused scandal. Such destruction was, moreover, dangerous, for it fostered civic riots and sedition, which worried Luther very much by 1525 because his reform was blamed for precisely such disturbances. Although he feared that images might promote works-righteousness, they could be of use to Christians "weak in faith." He later gradually moved from a cautious acceptance of images to attributing a positive value to them. Images were in themselves indifferent—to be used or not used insofar as they helped or hindered faith. That images might be beautiful does not enter the discussion.

By 1524 Karlstadt was arguing for destruction and against waiting for official approval. The matter was too urgent. Individuals and communities had to take matters into their own hands and remove or smash the offending articles. Karlstadt gave license for the many outbursts of Iconoclastic violence in the sixteenth century that were spontaneous and perhaps therefore particularly barbarous. In this he differed very much from mainline Reformers like Zwingli, Bullinger, and Calvin, who insisted that the removal and destruction of images be done only by lawful authority. By their vehement denunciations of idols in their sermons, however, preachers on both sides in fact encouraged violence.

Whether done lawfully or unlawfully, the end result was pretty much the same. All at once the material culture of Christianity in the West was in crisis. In many places Christians, no matter how little they cared about or comprehended the lofty theological battles being waged, awoke one morning to find themselves in a place of worship that looked utterly different from what they and their forebears for generations had been used to. When this occurred, it usually marked a point of no return regarding the old faith.

In Zurich under Zwingli's inspiration the transformation began on June 20, 1524, and was completed in two weeks. Every church was in orderly fashion cleared of statues, paintings, altar furnishings, votive lamps, and choir stalls. The walls were whitewashed. The scene was different five years later at St. Gall where the magistrates, in an act of legalized vandalism, encouraged the people to storm the churches and destroy what they found within. The cathedral alone produced forty-six wagons of rubble, which was hauled to a nearby square to be burned. In Scotland later in the century the devastation was almost total. Virtually nothing would remain of the artistic heritage of the nation.

Not only images were under attack but also the traditional rites and rituals of worship itself, including of course the vessels, furnishings, and vestments that were an integral part of them. The war against "idolatry" and the war against "ceremonies" were just two aspects of the same onslaught, as Karlstadt's example makes clear. According to Karlstadt, if images were idolatrous, so was the mass. It was to be replaced by a scriptural commemoration of the Last Supper, which required neither altar nor priest for it was not a sacrifice. On December 3, 1521, a mob inspired by Karlstadt forced its way into a church, destroyed the liturgical books, and drove the priest from the altar. The next day another mob destroyed the altar in the Franciscan cloister. Several weeks later, on Christmas day, Karlstadt performed the first reformed Eucharistic service in Wittenberg, wearing no vestments and addressing his flock as fellow laymen. When the next month the town council issued its statutes mandating change, it put the matter succinctly: "Both images and altars in churches are to be removed in order to avoid the idolatry that such altars and images promote."[33]

The attack was ultimately an attack on the sacramental principle of the invisible being mediated through visible objects and performance. More specifically, the attack on the mass was an attack on the Real Presence of Christ in the Eucharist. The mass, nothing more in this perspective than an adoration of bread and wine, was thus as idolatrous as adoration of a painted canvas. Karlstadt represented an extreme in this regard, but there was a direct correlation between how present or absent the Reformers considered Christ to be in the Eucharist and how moderately or radically they modified the mass in its medieval form, if they did not eliminate it altogether. The Anglicans and the Lutherans fall clearly on the traditional side, the Calvinists were much more radical, and the Anabaptists more radical still.

The sixteenth-century crisis was a crisis in "communal, performative signs."[34] It sprang from a mentality that saw ritual observances as a diversion from the truly spiritual or, even worse, as a manipulative fraud. Even in the Protestant churches, however, it did not result in the elimination of ritual or the total banishment of all art: "The image-breakers became image-makers."[35] Calvin, adamant and uncompromising about the removal of religious images from churches, allowed even biblical scenes in homes or in secular public buildings if they had some educational value. Luther pointed out that Iconoclasts read his German Bible, in which there were many pictures "both of God, the angels, men and animals."[36]

Lutherans removed many but not all images from their churches. Their service, still often referred to as mass, retained the traditional structure. Although now in the vernacular, it also commonly used Latin for parts sung by a boys' choir. Luther wanted to eliminate pomp and luxury from the service, yet he allowed freedom regarding vestments, so that some Lutheran churches later in the century had elegant ones. He was eager to turn the mass into an even more impressive musical event than he found it. He instructed that in every mass the words be sung, which included the Epistle and the Gospel of the day. Luther himself collected and composed hymns for the use of the congregation. No organs were removed from Lutheran churches. Although the role of the other arts suffered a diminution, music not only survived but greatly prospered. Johann Sebastian Bach is almost a second founder of the Lutheran tradition.

In Zurich Zwingli forbade all music in church. The organs, silenced in 1524, were destroyed in 1527. With most of the other reformers music fared best among the arts. Of the senses they showed special favor to hearing. After all, it was through hearing that the Word of God was received. The ear was the sense that opened the soul to the divine, the eye only to the human and the carnal. The ear seemed, as well, somehow more in accord with the call to interiority.

With the Book of Common Prayer, 1549, the liturgies of the Church of England—the mass, the Hours, the Burial Service—received a formulation that through many vicissitudes has retained its official status and its stately beauty up to the present. The Prayerbook, of relatively modest size, is remarkable for containing provisions for the whole liturgy, absorbing materials earlier contained in the Breviary (of the Hours), the Missal, and even the Processional. It achieved this feat by radical surgery, simplifying every aspect of the medieval forms. The eight Hours of the Office, for instance, were by a process of dismemberment and redistribution organized into just two, corresponding roughly to Lauds and Vespers—now, Morning Prayer and Evensong. Despite the drastic reduction in size and the Protestant influences, the continuity of the Book of Common Prayer with the immediately preceding tradition is strong. The Prayerbook has always been published without music, yet even with the dissolution of religious houses and other foundations that were able to sustain a sung liturgy, a strong musical tradition continued and developed in the Anglican church, with Byrd and Tallis leading the way. Later came Handel with "Saul," "Israel in Egypt," "Samson," and, glorious, "The Messiah."

Even in churches where the sacramental principle was more radically challenged, ritual could not be eliminated altogether. Human communities cannot exist, it seems, without ritual, no matter how meager or understated it is. Zwingli thought that the only true worship was done alone in the privacy of one's heart, averring that "worship is corrupted and vitiated by the many," but even he realized that some communal service was proper.[37] Moreover, did not baptism require the pouring of water?

Unlike their European counterparts, Protestants in the English colonies of North America had to build new churches. Even today in New England there are more than five hundred churches or meeting houses built before 1830, most of them embodying a clean and bright elegance, some with considerable ornamentation especially on the chief liturgical center, the pulpit. In the wake of the various Protestant reformations, therefore, vast quantities of old rituals were summarily tossed into the dustbin, new rituals created, some older ones reinterpreted and their relationship to the arts given a new orientation. The assaults eventually ended. Art and performance remained.

Although within the Reformation attitudes toward ritual and images covered a wide range, even the most conservative among them profoundly challenged Catholicism. A response had to be made. Behind Protestant actions lay words, and it was to those words that Catholics in the first instance responded. Karlstadt's attack on images appeared in January 1522. Two months later Hieronymus Emser published his refutation, twice as long as Karlstadt's work. In the style of the day, Emser laced his prose with sarcasm and contempt and accused Karlstadt of resurrecting the heresies of Wycliffe and Hus. In the first part he provided reasons why the church fostered images, which included the fact that portraits of the Virgin Mary painted by Saint Luke had come down to us. In general, however, he argued his case well and made good use of the line from the first chapter of Romans: "Ever since the creation of the world his invisible nature, namely, his eternal power and deity, has been clearly perceived in the things that have been made." He was reasonably well informed about the Second Council of Nicaea, and he quoted John Damascene.

In the second of his two parts he undertook a direct refutation of Karlstadt, quoting verbatim short passages before launching his rebuttal. Emser held several university degrees, including a bachelor's in theology, but he was also much influenced by the humanist movement. He was therefore at home in both of those bookish cultures. For that reason when he accuses Karlstadt of accepting from books what he will not accept from images, he makes one of his most effective points. The context is Karlstadt's attack on Gregory the Great's "Bible for the illiterate." Emser says: "Then Karlstadt mockingly asks and says, Tell me, dear Gregory, what good are the laity able to learn from pictures? Therefore, I ask Karlstadt in return, What good have he and his friends learned from books? Or, What more can the written word be than a sign that signifies and indicates something else, which is precisely what images do?" Karlstadt invoked the line from John's gospel about God being spirit, and Emser retorted, "But what John says concerns not only the laity with their images but also the learned with their books. For if God does not touch and attract our hearts, neither book nor image can help."[38]

Emser placed remarkably little emphasis on the didactic function of images. He was more concerned with their ability to stimulate virtue and devotion, which leads to imitation; with their ability to remind us of God and his benefits, and thus to help us be grateful; with their reminder of the intercession of the saints on our behalf; and with their ability to touch hearts in a particularly effective way. He defended their veneration through the lighting of candles and similar practices, but he avoided saying anything about miraculous images.

Quoting Erasmus favorably, he conceded that it was better to give to the poor and the needy from the money one might expend for a candle or for an image, but, if one had the means, why not do both? At the tomb on the day of Christ's resurrection the angel did not reprove the three Marys because they had spent so much money for ointment for Christ's body, even though the angel knew that it was of no use since he was no longer in the grave.

Johann Eck was Luther's first and most formidable early opponent. His treatise appeared about the same time as Emser's and was a reaction not so much to Karlstadt as to the actual removal of crucifixes and images of the saints from the churches of Ingolstadt, which he discovered when he returned there from a trip to Rome. The treatise, structured as a set of theses, covers much the same ground as Emser. The first of his theses is the most fundamental: "Through the incarnation of the Word, the invisible God was made visible and capable of being represented."[39]

Throughout the century Catholics continued to publish works defending images, but without doubt the most important statement on the matter was the decree of the Council of Trent, ratified and published on the last day of the council, December 4, 1563. Not until mid-November, just two weeks before the council ended, was a commission of five bishops and five theologians put to work on a decree to deal with the cult of the saints and the veneration of relics and images. The late date testifies to the immense difficulties the council experienced in dealing with almost every aspect of "reform," but it also suggests that the matter was deemed of lesser importance than "doctrine" and even "discipline." Until the arrival of the French bishops in November 1562, almost all the participants in the council were from Italy or Iberia, which had not experienced any notable destruction of images, whereas in France at just that time Iconoclasm had violently erupted in a number of cities. It is not surprising, therefore, that the commission held its meetings in the residence of the Cardinal of Lorraine, Charles de Guise, the leader of the French delegation.

The council was rushing to finish its business, and the decree was put together in haste. Because of the press of time, the text on images was never publicly debated, and no documents relating to it are to be found in the proceedings of the council. Even under these circumstances, the decree turned out to be a balanced and concise summary of traditional thinking, worthy of culture two. Explicitly referring to the Second Council of Nicaea, it defended images and their veneration, as with kisses and the bowing of the head, for what is honored is not the material object but the prototype for which it stands. Images teach, they excite devotion and love of God, they remind of benefits, and they incite to imitation of Christ and the saints. Bishops should encourage placing images of Christ and the saints in churches as well as in other places.

The text says nothing about images being aesthetically pleasing. It warned, however, that they should not depict any false doctrine and that their veneration should be free of superstition and anything lascivious. The bishop's permission was required for the installation of any "unusual" image in churches. For this specific instance the decree thus legislated censorship of images depicting sacred subjects. Except for those "unusual" images the decree did not specify further, but it opened the door for bishops, inquisitors, and theologians after the council to move in to ensure that paintings were historically, doctrinally, and morally correct, a determining factor in producing the so-called Tridentine art of the next several decades, the decades of the "severe morality" that held much of both Catholic and Protestant Europe in its tight grip.

Yet even with its warning about possible abuses and its threat of interference, the decree had resolutely affirmed the validity and importance of images. Let churches and other places be adorned with them! It was a message, certainly not unexpected, that fell sweetly on the ears of artists and their patrons and that removed a potential obstacle to their enterprise.

Simply by leaving the basic structure of the mass unchanged and strongly asserting the Real Presence of Christ under the appearance of bread and wine, the council had important repercussions for liturgical performance. This is even more obviously true for its explicit affirmation of the legitimacy and desirability "of ceremonies, such as mystical blessings, lights, incense, vestments and many other things of this kind in accordance with apostolic usage and tradition, whereby both the majesty of so great a sacrifice might be enhanced and the minds of the faithful lifted up by visible signs of religion and piety to the contemplation of the mysteries hidden in it." With regard to music it said only that bishops were to banish anything "lascivious or impure."[40] It made no statement about church architecture, but in two places it put bishops under obligation to repair the material fabric of the churches that needed it.

Baroque Celebration

With the council the theologians had their say. They extended their hands to culture four in a cautious gesture of friendship. But culture four had a powerful energy of its own that carried it forward in new outbursts of productivity. Beleaguered and belittled by prestigious adversaries earlier on, it responded in its own terms simply by doing its own thing, producing beautiful forms, but doing so perhaps more copiously and more exuberantly than it had in a long time, if ever. Culture four found itself at the center of society with a predominance as impressive as it had enjoyed in Roman antiquity. By the seventeenth century it was aided in this achievement by the renewed bonds of mutual assistance between itself and especially culture three, as poetry, oratory, and the arts celebrated together their partnership.

What is remarkable is the madness for painting, sculpture, and a wide variety of architectural forms—villas, palaces, churches, and other public buildings—that seized seemingly all those who had the means to patronize them. Outside the religious sphere—in royal and ducal courts, in municipalities, in the ever more opulent households of great families and the upper bourgeoisie—culture four forged ahead, in both Catholic and Protestant territories, with energies long active in the Western tradition driving it along with renewed force. Secular subjects—portraits, landscapes, mythological gods and scenes—became ever more common for the figurative arts, and grand edifices dedicated to worldly pursuits and pleasures were erected in abundance.

The prelatial and princely courts of the *ancien régime* articulated rituals ever more formal and elaborate. To enhance them and to inspire respect for the exalted personages at their apogee, the courts produced and patronized art and artifacts in prodigious abundance and in an impressive multiplicity of forms—buildings, tapestries, paintings, and sculptures of course, but also thousands of smaller objects like tableware and figurines.

Even as clearer distinctions were being made in certain spheres between the sacred and the secular, the imagery and forms of courtly rituals were nonetheless often religiously derived, in Protestant courts as well as Catholic. Such imagery was projected by the courts' material culture. The chapel was, in theory at least, the epicenter of the court. Music was crucially important there as elsewhere in the palace. When the court was Catholic, the chapel provided yet another place and occasion for the installation of paintings, sculptures, and tapestries, as well as for the display of costly liturgical vestments, richly bejeweled reliquaries, processional crosses, monstrances, and similar objects peculiar to the Catholic cult.

The single most important wellspring and engine for the astounding production of material culture in the early modern era, however, was the church itself in its Roman Catholic form. The decree of Trent on sacred images was surely important in that it validated the enterprise and encouraged it. How directly it touched artists and their patrons varied considerably over the next century, even to the point of seeming in many instances not to have touched them at all. Other factors were powerfully at work.

Perhaps more important than the decree on images was Trent's injunction to bishops to repair and restore churches in their dioceses. Visiting churches was a crucial element in the "reform" the bishops were to effect, and an important task of the visitation was to see to the care, repair, and upkeep of the physical fabric. Especially in Italy many bishops took this task seriously, providing money for artists and architects and space for them in which to exercise their art. The bishops thus instituted in a newly intentional way a responsibility traditional for the public man of the *paideia.*

The civic aspect of this responsibility that moved beyond ecclesiastical edifices was dramatically illustrated in Rome, where the bishop still ruled the city. In the late sixteenth and early seventeenth centuries a spectacular refashioning of the city, under way since the early fifteenth century but somewhat stalled in the middle decades of the sixteenth, took off with incredible energy and resulted in the laying out of streets and piazzas, the creation of fountains, the erection of obelisks and public statuary—all done with an eye to public ritual and performance.

But besides the bishops Catholicism had among its resources the new religious orders that had come into being in the sixteenth century—the Barnabites, the Theatines, the Oratorians, the Capuchins, and the Jesuits. Operating independent of the bishops, they were all soon engaged in extensive building programs, undertaken often in an ill-concealed rivalry with one another. The bishops generally restored old churches. These orders built new ones. They employed the best architects and artists they or their patrons could afford. The first of these churches to be built was the Jesuits' Gesù in Rome, funded by the powerful Farnese cardinals and designed principally by Vignola. It is generally considered the most important church building erected in the early modern era. It helped stimulate the Theatines to build their Sant' Andrea della Valle, the Oratorians their Chiesa Nuova, the Barnabites their San Carlo ai Catinari—all within a short walk of one another.

The Jesuits were particularly important because of the large number of recruits they attracted and because of the international character of the order since its founding. Everywhere in the world they went they built churches and usually large school complexes to go with them. Whatever their motives, they sought not only to install large numbers of paintings in their churches but sometimes also to cover the walls of their own residences with them. At their novitiate at Sant' Andrea al Quirinale in Rome, for instance, for which Bernini would later construct the chapel, every space of every room in the infirmary was frescoed, including the ceiling, with each room having its own theme.

Between 1580 and 1650 in Bavaria alone, where the Jesuits had a foothold from the earliest days of the order, they built twenty-four new churches and renovated at least nine others, to say nothing of the oratories, shrine churches, and academic buildings they erected or restored. In most of these structures they of course installed new organs and hired organists and other musicians. *Sensual Worship* is the apt title of the most recent book on the subject.[41]

The older orders like the Dominicans and the Franciscans already had their churches in Europe. They lost many to the Reformation, often in places where there was little hope of reestablishing themselves, but they had wide scope for building in Latin America, the Philippines, and elsewhere outside Europe. The missionaries requisitioned from Europe great quantities of oil paintings, tapestries, illustrated printed books, vestments, and objects d'art. In 1564 Luis Fróis, a Jesuit missionary in Japan, reported that more than fifty thousand devotional images were needed to satisfy the growing Christian community there. A short while later Jesuits in Japan established an academy for training Europeans and Japanese in oil and watercolor painting, copper engraving, and the production of bronze plaquettes and sculpture. Training in singing and the playing of musical instruments was included in the program.

But surely fundamental to the production of material culture in such extraordinary quantity and quality was the fact that Italy, Flanders, and Spain were Catholic. In pre-Reformation Europe Italy and Flanders were the two great centers of production, homes to the greatest artists and architects, in contexts where the creation of the beautiful was of highest priority. They continued to be so in the early modern era, with Spain now experiencing many flashes of brilliance. Especially in Italy the supply of artists of the highest quality seemed inexhaustible. If bishops and religious orders needed new churches and art to fill them, if devout laity wanted chapels, altar pieces, and devotional pictures, the supply was more than sufficient to meet the demand—and to help create the demand. If wealthy patrons wanted their portraits painted or the ceilings of their great salons frescoed, they had at hand an abundance of artists of the utmost skill to do their bidding.

Erasmus and the theologians of Trent would not have been pleased with the fleshly turn painting and sculpture took even for religious subjects in the baroque era, when Caravaggio, Bernini, and Rubens were the stars. For these artists and their patrons, many of whom were bishops, cardinals, and sometimes popes, the warning against lasciviousness of the Council of Trent had for one reason or another become inoperative. True, Caravaggio's Madonna dei Palafrenieri, with its full frontal nudity of the boy Jesus, was rejected by the papal groomsmen who commissioned it for their chapel in the new Saint Peter's, but it was immediately snapped up by Cardinal Scipione Borghese. Rubens's Holy Family with Saint Anne, originally located in the monastery of San Lorenzo in the Escorial, is centered on a frontally nude infant Jesus, whose right hand rests on his mother's exposed breast while his left caresses her neck. Mary Magdalen continued to be a favored subject, depicted by all three of these artists, and she was, even in her penitence, ever more sensually portrayed. Bernini's sculpture of her, nude, is located in a niche in the cathedral in Siena.

If the seventeenth century witnessed a renewed partnership among the three "Athenian" cultures, the partnership manifested itself even in the training artists now wanted and to a large extent achieved for themselves. The change began to occur in the fifteenth century, when to better their social status as well as to further educate themselves a few of these "artisans" began to learn Latin. Knowledge of classical history and mythology became almost indispensable for obtaining and retaining the better patrons. Artists might try to gain entry to the intellectual's territory by writing poetry or even by writing about the theory and practice of their art. By the end of the fifteenth century knowledge of geometry, a subject of the ancient quadrivium, was a required skill for perspective composition.

Bronzino, like his older contemporary Michelangelo as well as others, composed poems worth the study. By the seventeenth century such a change had occurred in the education and status of artists that a virtuoso like Peter Paul Rubens brilliantly exemplified the Renaissance ideal of *uomo universale*—an avid reader of Latin literature, a profound student of Stoic philosophy, an archaeologist of talent, an assiduous collector of books, a successful diplomat in the service of his country, a faithful correspondent with notables across Europe, a devout Catholic who assisted at mass daily, and a friend and mentor to younger artists, including his most talented disciple, Anthony van Dyke.

The partnership among the cultures displayed itself visually and publicly in elaborate events and celebrations of various kinds. Rome with its great churches and the households of the cardinals was an especially splendid theater for performance and spectacle. But the enthusiasm found expression even in the strongholds of culture two. By the early seventeenth century the Jesuits' Roman College had become the outstanding educational institution in the city, outstripping even the much older University of Rome, known as La Sapienza. The "College" was a university, highly respected for its mathematicians and astronomers, as well as its professors of Scholastic theology and metaphysics. It also taught the "lower subjects" of grammar and rhetoric. Its student body consisted of not only young clerics but also many lay students, including scions of great families.

The academic calendar was punctuated with celebrations in which music, poetry, oratory, and performances of various kinds blended. Among these were public events in which especially successful students defended theses in Scholastic philosophy or theology, material solidly from culture two. These defenses were multimedia events of the highest order. For them the students in question wanted to attract a large and refined audience and were often willing to go to great expense to do so. The spectacles were lavish. The great aula was decorated with garlands and flowers and the walls hung with tapestries. Most often special music was composed for the occasion and performed at intervals throughout the examination by anywhere from one to eight separate choirs singing madrigals and motets. Instrumental music was provided by an orchestra, which might boast as many as four trumpets. Poetry, again composed for the occasion, was, when not set to music, recited as part of the celebration, which was a celebration, likely as not, of a principle of Aristotelian physics or metaphysics.

The program of the humanistic schools called for training in all aspects of civility, including music and dance. The statutes from 1548 for the Jesuit school in Coimbra stipulated that students suitable for it be taught singing for two hours every Sunday and feast day. In Rome some years later the Jesuits hired Palestrina and Tomás Luis de Victoria to teach their students. Much later in Paris they hired Marc-Antoine Charpentier for the same purpose. Beginning in 1622 they wrote or commissioned operas open to the public in which students performed alongside professional musicians. These were small, local manifestations of an era of masses and oratorios by musical geniuses from Palestrina to Haydn.

By the early seventeenth century the most prestigious Jesuit schools in Italy employed for their students a teacher of dance, *maestro di ballo.* Especially in France, the Jesuits schools became noted for dance. Once a year, for instance, at the showcase Collège Louis-le-Grand in Paris a "ballet" filled the intermission between acts of a play. Interspersed among the student dancers were often professionals hired for the purpose. In smaller colleges ballets were sometimes performed in the chapel, for lack of another sufficiently large space, to the great scandal of the Jansenists, who denounced the practice as sacrilege. Of the ten books on the history and theory of dance published in France between 1658 and 1760, six were by Jesuit teachers or writers. A Jesuit review of one of the books not by a Jesuit recommended it by saying it would make readers "feel something of the gaiety and playfulness that even the idea of dance naturally brings with it."[42]

The arts burst out of the confines of church, school, and court to continue and even intensify the great civic/religious spectacles of earlier eras and to engage all strata of society. Celebrations could last for days, or even weeks, as they did with typically baroque exuberance in Manila in the early 1620s after the papacy had approved for the whole church the public observance of the feast of the Immaculate Conception. When the news reached Manila, city officials set aside nineteen days for celebration. In conjunction with the civic notables the churches mounted a program that seemed to know no limits. Fireworks were set off every night. The cathedral was the center for the festivities, but every religious institution played an important role.

The first day opened with a solemn polyphonic mass in the cathedral, followed in the afternoon by a play on the beauty of Rachel. The next day the Franciscans took over with a great procession through the city streets that included dancing along the way by one of the friars, eight floats containing statues of Franciscan saints, and each float accompanied by a group of Indian dancers. In the afternoon was a production of a play about the recent Christian martyrs in Japan. Wednesday was the Jesuits' day, with mass and other events done with "a thousand musical instruments." On Saturday evening the Jesuits organized a procession headed by three triumphal chariots—the first accompanied by clarion players, the second by singers doing motets and ballads, and the third by players of a variety of musical instruments. The procession included eight children dressed in silk garments and carrying candles in silver holders, singing hymns in praise of the Virgin. On the last day a dance was performed by more than sixty Japanese Christians who, accompanied by instrumental music, sang while they danced. The inhabitants of Manila carried on this way every day for almost three weeks.

Art and Performance Prevail

The Enlightenment and the French Revolution were watersheds for culture four, which in the nineteenth and twentieth centuries would look astoundingly different from how it had looked in all the preceding eras. Aesthetic taste shifted radically, perhaps nowhere more ubiquitously visible than in the way men in the West have since dressed. The more solemn the occasion, the more sober the dress. No plumes, no trains, no brocade waistcoats, no lace cuffs, and, heavens, no codpieces. Women's fashions changed in the same way, though slightly less drastically and prescriptively.

By the latter years of the nineteenth century faith in artistic and ritual standards derived in some discernible way from the world of Athens had clearly eroded here, too, as it had eroded in different spheres of cultures two and three: "We do not care for Raphael."[43] Museums in North America would eventually be eager to acquire notable collections of Asian and African art, which contain some of their most admired pieces.

The gaze fixed on the future or outside the Euro-American world meant a gaze turned perhaps even more resolutely away from Jerusalem than from Athens, that is, away from the Bible and traditions deriving from it. In the production of culture four any relationship with sacred subjects and occasions began to disappear almost completely.

The churches no longer acted as the great patrons, partly because the economic base had slipped for prelates and the like in the course of the nineteenth and twentieth centuries. In both Catholic and Protestant churches, moreover, disdain for "the modern world," and hence "modern art," was widespread. As the nineteenth century wore on, Catholic bishops and their counterparts in Protestant churches were drawn less and less often from aristocratic families, which by tradition of their milieu took their patronage of culture four as a given. A new, supposedly more pastoral, ideal of the clergyman was also emerging in which the arts got little attention.

The texture of public ritual became more secular and, at least for serious occasions, more subdued. The ritual for the inauguration of a president of the United States is dignified and in its stark simplicity reflects and suggests values deeply rooted in the American political ethos. But it looks so different from a medieval or baroque coronation rite as to be incomparable. As with presidential inaugurations and football rallies, most other rituals outside the religious sphere are enacted with minimal or at least greatly reduced engagement of the arts. Symbols, those inseparable companions to rituals, are, like rituals themselves, rarely recognized as such even though they abound everywhere. Every business company has its logo.

Christian churches even in the post-baroque, indeed postmodern, era do not labor under that last disability. They know they use symbols, and they know they engage in ritual. Despite the relative absence of the churches from the world of art, on great festival days the artistic engagement can be impressive. A solemn liturgy in Westminster Abbey and a rousing one in an Afro-American frame church are both deeply moving, owing in large measure to the way the arts are integrated into them. In the case of the latter, it is amazing how many of the best-known and most respected singers of both classical and popular music got their start in the church choir.

But in our era culture four tends to stand on its own, unintegrated into a larger scene, though a huge exception must perhaps be made for its popular forms, commercialized though they often are. In earlier times what we consider "serious" painting, sculpture, music, and dance were located in places and rituals where they were not something to be enjoyed apart, whereas now they are found in edifices or occasions set aside exclusively for them. They are "works of art." They were produced by "artists" and for the most part independent of occasions. Instead of being located in churches, courts, processions, and public celebrations of various kinds, popular as well as elite, they are found in museums and concert halls (or on compact disks), where they are to be admired and enjoyed for their own sake. "Art" has a place in the lives of educated people, but its place is not where they live, work, or, often, even where they worship. It is a place to which they go, for a visit.

Finally, the practitioners of culture four are trained differently than in the past. In antiquity and the Middle Ages their mentors were their fathers or grandfathers. Later practitioners organized themselves into self-regulating guilds, which in the early modern period developed into academies. Today artists, architects, and musicians are trained in formal schools, which are often part of a much larger institution, a university. This means deans, degrees, and diplomas, and it means examinations and grades—a haven for culture four but in an establishment governed by the values of culture two.

Even with all these changes culture four is still culture four, powerfully present among us and creative, lifting us (we know not how or why) to another world. Bernstein and Sondheim, Balanchine and Alvin Ailey, O'Keeffe and Pollock, Frank Lloyd Wright and Frank Gehry. Countless pop stars. Art and performance prevail in all their high and low forms, in all their modern and postmodern styles, in all the serious and not-so-serious play into which they entice us.